Realistic Animation, Lighting & Sound

— SECOND EDITION —

KALMBACH BOOKS

Kalmbach Books
21027 Crossroads Circle
Waukesha, Wisconsin 53186
www.Kalmbach.com/Books

Published in 2012
16 15 14 13 12   1 2 3 4 5

Manufactured in the United States of America

ISBN: 978-0-89024-863-8

Editor: Jeff Wilson
Art Director: Tom Ford

Publisher's Cataloging-In-Publication Data

Realistic animation, lighting & sound / [compiled by Kalmbach Books]. -- 2nd ed.

   p. : ill. (some col.) ; cm. -- (Model railroader books)

   "The projects in this book originally appeared as articles in Model Railroader magazine."--copyright page.
   ISBN: 9780890248638

   1. Railroads--Models--Design and construction--Handbooks, manuals, etc. 2. Models and modelmaking--Handbooks, manuals, etc. I. Kalmbach Publishing Company. II. Title: Realistic animation, lighting and sound III. Title: Model Railroader magazine. IV. Series: Model railroader books.

TF197 .R42 2012
625.1/9

Contents

Photos by George Hall

1

Animation on the Lone Pine & Tonopah

By Kermit Paul and Ken Sullivan

The Sullivan Lumber Co., scratchbuilt by Ken Sullivan, has an operating drag chain that pulls logs into the mill, spinning saw blades, a movable saw carriage, and a "green" chain where the finished lumber is delivered and graded.

Animation is a combination of mechanical and lighting effects that give the appearance of purposeful motion. While some of our examples may seem complex, all of these devices break down into simple applications of basic principles.

Quiet, slow-speed geared motors are the heart of all these animation devices. Their slow rotary motion can be converted to linear (back-and-forth) or angular motion, **1**. When rotary motion is necessary, it can be transmitted using cams, chains and sprockets, or belts and pulleys.

I use mechanical animation to operate a number of devices on my HO scale LP&T:
- Dancers moving inside the USO dance hall
- Log dump at the mill pond
- Log loader in the woods
- Moving automobiles
- Rocker-style oil pumps
- Rotating oil and water spouts for locomotives
- Sawmill carriage, saws, and log chain
- Scrap-metal loading crane
- Semaphore signals

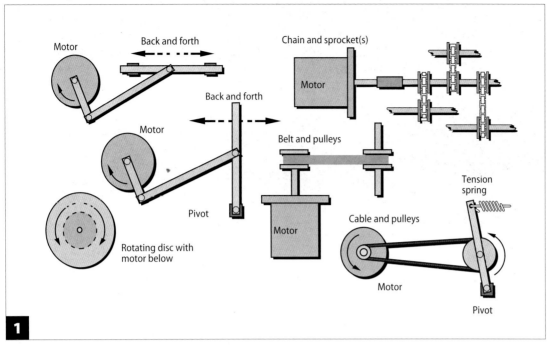

Motion can be transferred from a motor to models in several ways.

Motion can also be created by using flashing or flickering lights to simulate fires, arc welders, emergency vehicle lights, traffic lights, and similar items. By sequencing the lights, it's possible to reproduce industrial signs and theater chase lights. Examples of these lighting effects are incorporated into:

- Day-to-night changes in the layout room lighting
- Hobo campfire
- House on fire
- Neon signs
- Sawdust burner
- Theater chase lights
- Traffic lights
- USO dance hall's jukebox

Material sources

Most animation materials you'll need are available from model railroad hobby sources. Slow-speed Hankscraft geared motors are sold under the brand names of Switchmaster and American Switch & Signal, although I've found similar motors in surplus stores and at hobby flea markets. The chain and sprockets are marketed by Grandt Line and industrial gear suppliers. Drive belts are available in video repair kits sold by electronic suppliers. K&S sells brass bars, rods, and tubing useful for bearings, shafts, and supports.

Dancers

Build a dance hall so its entire floor is a plastic disk that slowly rotates, with figures attached to it. The floor isn't visible, so the movement produces an illusion of dancing couples. Top it off with an acrylic plastic jukebox and illuminate it through a rotating disk of multicolored lenses. A tape or CD player and concealed speaker provide appropriate dance music.

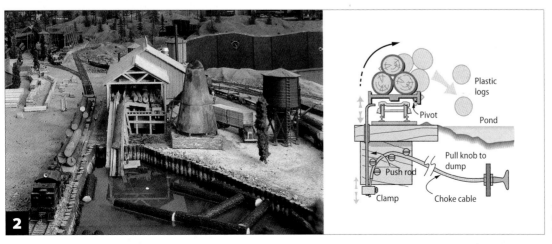

A choke cable enables log cars to be dumped.

A pair of motors enables the log boom to turn as well as raise and lower.

Log dump

Figure **2** shows the device that dumps logs off flatcars and into a pond filled with real water. Pulling an automobile choke cable lifts a brass rod to tip the flatcar deck and dump the logs.

The special flatcars I use were originally marketed by Cox (no longer made), and the same cars were also sold under the old AHM label. A little paint and weathering does wonders on them. These cars come with three hollow plastic logs that float.

Log loading boom and sawmill

Figure **3** shows the log boom that loads flatcars at the lumber camp. The spar pole is cut into two sections just below the boom. A brass bearing tube runs down through the fixed lower section and into the layout. A smaller-diameter brass rod is attached to the upper section so it extends down through the fixed lower portion. One motor, concealed under the bench top, rotates the rod to shift the boom from side to side.

A second motor raises and lowers the counter-weighted main cable, which comes up through a dummy donkey engine and over the pulleys on the boom. A pair of weighted dummy cables, one on each side, gives the illusion that the boom is being rotated by the donkey engine. Add a Märklin electromagnet, detailed with log jaws, to the main cable to handle the logs.

Kadee's plastic logs can be modified for magnetic pickup. Roll a 1"-wide strip of tin into a tube that fits snugly inside the log. Center the tin tube within the log, secure it with cyanoacrylate adhesive (CA), and glue the plastic ends in place. The magnet is strong enough to attract the tin through the thin log wall, while the log remains light enough to float.

Sawmills have lots of interesting action that can be animated, **1**. Make a drag chain to pull logs from the pond into the mill from Andeco plastic chain

and matching sprockets from Grandt Line. It's driven by a single Hankscraft motor. Attach small pins to the plastic chain so they catch and push the logs up into the sawmill. Once they're out of sight inside the mill, the logs drop through a hole and into a collection box hidden beneath the layout. The large circular saws may be simulated with a pair of Dremel saw blades mounted on belt-driven horizontal shafts and run by a single motor.

Use a Hankscraft motor to operate a slider-crank and spring-loaded cable to move the log carriage back and forth in front of the rotating saw blades. To complete the illusion, mount a partially cut log on the carriage so its flat side faces the blades.

Two matching loops of Andeco chain, driven by a single motor, make an excellent miniature "green chain" for the sawmill. Tiny pins on the chains carry the freshly cut boards past the sorter, who grades and stacks them at the finishing end of the mill.

Action can also be added inside the conical sawdust burner by using flickering red and yellow lights. GRS Micro-Liting and others make ready-to-use simulated-fire effects.

Moving automobiles

Moving vehicles always capture attention, **4**. On the LP&T, a continuous loop of model airplane multi-strand control line cable runs in a thin slot built into the pavement. Small pins, silver-soldered to the metal cable at irregular intervals, extend above the slot to pull autos along the street.

The drawing in **4** shows a cross section of the street with cable slots fabricated from code 100 rail soldered to brass crossties. The thin gap between the railheads allows the vertical pins to pass, but keeps the cable from lifting out of the slot. Soldering ⅛" lengths of ¹⁄₁₆" brass tubing to the cable at 12" intervals helps keep the cable within the slot.

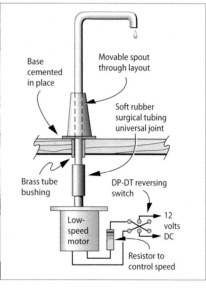

4

Road centerline

Width to allow vehicles to pass

Section at A-A

Paired code 100 rails

Pin to pull vehicle

Section at B-B

Cable with retainer

Pavement

Moving vehicles are pulled along by pins attached to a metal cable. The cable is guided along a slot made by a pair of rails placed side by side.

5

Base cemented in place

Movable spout through layout

Soft rubber surgical tubing universal joint

Brass tube bushing

DP-DT reversing switch

Low-speed motor

12 volts DC

Resistor to control speed

A low-speed motor enables oil or water spouts to turn as needed when servicing locomotives.

Install heavy-duty slow-speed motors with identical drive pulleys at both ends of the street. One motor and pulley set should be stationary; the other motor needs a spring-loaded mounting to maintain tension on the cable. Determine the cable loop's length, cut off the excess, and then silver-solder the splice for maximum strength.

Vehicles need free-rolling axles. Drill a small hole into the chassis just ahead of the front axle to fit over the cable pins. Test-run the device, make any necessary adjustments, and build the street surface.

Neon lights and signs

Chapter 20 shows a couple of methods for simulating neon signs. Neon store-window sign kits were made in numerous designs by Quality Products Co., Miller Engineering, and Miniatronics. Some of these signs include blinking effects.

Lighted jewelry is another source of neon signs. I found a battery-operated brooch, about 1¾" tall,

with a green palm tree and orange trunk (other patterns can also be found). A built-in switch allows continuous or flashing operation. Mount the light into the side of a building and add appropriate lettering around it. On the LP&T, the brooch marks "The Green Palm Club," **4**.

Rotating fuel oil and water spouts

You can use a Hankscraft motor mounted beneath the layout to swing an oil or water spout over either service track, **5**. Use soft surgical tubing for the coupling so a locomotive can push the spout out of the way in case someone leaves it fouling the service track.

Scrap-metal loading crane

The crane loading scrap metal, **6**, requires a mechanism similar to the log loader. Mount the crane cab on a ³⁄₁₆" brass tube that rotates in a telescoping tube bushing cemented into the layout. One Hankscraft motor rotates the cab with a belt drive; two others

Motors allow turning and controlling the boom on this scrapyard crane, and an electromagnet allows it to pick up simulated scrap loads.

Motors mounted on bracket attached to center tube

Hoist motor

Epoxy center tube to cab

Rotation motor

Belt drive

Boom motor

Bushing cemented to crane track, and benchtop

6

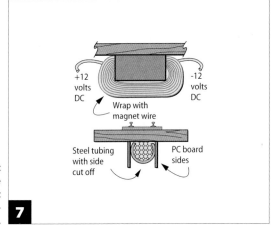

An electromagnetic coupler can be made by wrapping magnet wire around a steel-tubing core.

+12 volts DC

-12 volts DC

Wrap with magnet wire

Steel tubing with side cut off

PC board sides

7

raise and lower the boom and operate the hoist cable. Mount both motors on the cab rotation tube so they turn with it to minimize cable problems.

A Märklin electromagnet handles the scrap metal. Simulate baled steel scrap by gluing bits of tin to blocks of balsa wood and wrap the blocks in crushed aluminum foil. Once they're painted and weathered, the blocks look like crushed and baled automobiles.

Electromagnetic uncouplers

Hidden electric uncouplers are handy if you use magnetic knuckle couplers. You can make a concealed electromagnetic uncoupler that can be controlled with a push button, **7**. This device has a 2"-long electromagnet that creates a strong magnetic field across the track. It really snaps the coupler knuckles open and easily shifts the coupler into the delayed uncoupling position once the couplers are separated.

Use a piece of 1" steel tubing with one side cut off to form the core. Attach a pair of side pieces, made of printed-circuit-board material, to the core. Wrap enameled magnet wire lengthwise around the core until it's filled. The wire size is a matter of choice; fine wire requires more turns and a higher DC oper-

ating voltage, but it uses less current. Mount the coil so the cut edges of the steel core are just below the ties and rails. When it's actuated, the magnetic field will open the coupler knuckles. Mark the center of the concealed uncoupler with a dab of paint on a tie.

Use a heavy-duty push button to control the coil, and connect a diode across the coil to suppress the voltage "kick" when the button is released. Don't use the small Radio Shack red push buttons: they aren't adequate for this application.

Sunset and sunrise

To achieve the full benefit of special layout lighting effects, you'll want to dim the layout room lighting. Use incandescent lighting arranged in several circuits on lamp dimmers. They're available as dining-room dimmers at most large hardware stores.

Since this involves potentially lethal 110-volt electrical power, get professional help for this step if you're not familiar with such work and the local electrical code.

Mount the dimmers next to each other with their control shafts geared together. Drive the setup with a slow-speed motor that takes several minutes for full rotation. For the sunset sequence, run the motor and turn the dimmers down until the room lights are almost extinguished. Use a limit switch to turn the motor off so the lamp filaments are left barely glowing. Then the motor can be reversed for a gradual sunrise. Turning the dimmer back on, if the filaments are completely off, defeats the gradual sunrise as the lamps will suddenly "snap" to partial brilliance.

Animation is an opportunity that's still evolving in the hobby. Materials are readily available and construction methods and mechanics are easy to master. Once you have experienced the realism of animation, you'll be looking at nearly everything on your layout from a different perspective.

Photos by the author

Build a working wig-wag signal

2

By Woody Langley

At the dawn of the 20th century Americans rapidly converted from horses to automobiles. Horses had always been pretty good at looking out for themselves, but the same couldn't be said for motorists. The old "watch out for the trains" signs were no longer sufficient to protect railroad crossings, so flagmen, flashing lights, and warning bells were introduced.

The wig-wag is born

One device, developed by J. B. Hunt of southern California's Pacific Electric Ry., was an electro-mechanical hybrid of all three of these methods. The PE called it an "automatic flagman"; the more popular name was "wig-wag."

Between 1910 and 1920, the PE placed 117 automatic flagmen in service. These early versions were powered by electric motors, but excessive maintenance costs prompted an ingenious redesign. The motorized mechanism was replaced by an offset pair of electromagnets that alternately attracted an iron bar attached to the target shaft. With far fewer moving parts, there was less to wear out or break.

Two old-timers watch a "Big Red" car on the author's HO layout. The prototype signal on the Eureka Southern is still wagging after all these years, but it looks like the target has gotten bent. This signal is mounted atop a relay case, as was frequently done.

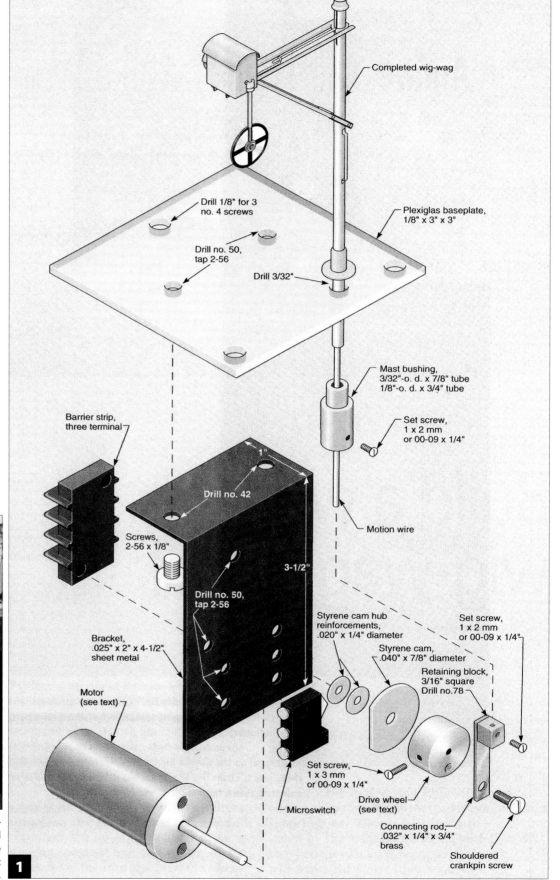

Completed wig-wag

Plexiglas baseplate,
1/8" x 3" x 3"

Drill 1/8" for 3
no. 4 screws

Drill no. 50,
tap 2-56

Drill 3/32"

Mast bushing,
3/32"-o. d. x 7/8" tube
1/8"-o. d. x 3/4" tube

Set screw,
1 x 2 mm
or 00-09 x 1/4"

Barrier strip,
three terminal

1"

Drill no. 42

Screws,
2-56 x 1/8"

3-1/2"

Drill no. 50,
tap 2-56

Motion wire

Set screw,
1 x 2 mm
or 00-09 x 1/4"

Styrene cam hub
reinforcements,
.020" x 1/4" diameter

Styrene cam,
.040" x 7/8" diameter

Retaining block,
3/16" square
Drill no.78

Bracket,
.025" x 2" x 4-1/2"
sheet metal

Motor
(see text)

Set screw,
1 x 3 mm
or 00-09 x 1/4"

Microswitch

Drive wheel
(see text)

Connecting rod,
.032" x 1/4" x 3/4"
brass

Shouldered
crankpin screw

Here's a finished wig-wag with the control mechanism visible under the layout table.

1

As of 1921 the PE had replaced all its original signals with electromagnetic models. By late 1926 about 500 of these were operating throughout the system. Bearing the trademark "Magnetic Flagman," these signals were manufactured by the Magnetic Signal Co. of Los Angeles. The Santa Fe, Southern Pacific, and other railroads also bought them.

Wig-wags have been a hardy breed, a testament to their elegantly simple, yet sound, design. Although no longer legal for new installations, a few could be found in operation into the 2000s.

The motor and microswitch

Scratchbuilding a working HO scale wig-wag isn't difficult, although it does require fabricating small parts from brass and soldering them together. I used a resistance soldering rig, but you'll do just fine with a conventional soldering iron. You can see a drawing of the whole system and a finished signal in **1**.

To power my wig-wag I chose a Faulhaber micromotor with a slip-on reduction gear head. These may no longer be available; look for a small DC motor that can be adjusted to about 42 rpm. Two possible sources are Micro Mo Electronics (www.micromo.com) and Micro-Mark (www.micromark.com).

Start by making a mounting bracket and attaching the motor to it, **2**. A homemade cam, mounted on the motor's drive shaft, engages a microswitch that won't allow the motor to stop running until the signal's target is hanging straight down.

I used draftsman's dividers to make the cam from .040" sheet styrene, **3**. My cam measures ⅞" in diameter, but that measurement isn't critical. The two reinforcement disks were added to increase the hub's grip on the motor shaft. I made these by drilling center holes in .020" styrene, then punching out the disks with a ¼" paper punch.

Press the cam on the shaft, then mount the microswitch. These are available at electronics stores. Two good ones for this project are the Cherry E63 or the GC Electronics 35-822. You want the cam just close enough so the switch clicks during the transitions between round and flat areas.

Mount the terminal strip on the opposite side of the bracket, **4**. I labeled my terminals COMMON, PLUS, and CONTROL. COMMON is the negative output from the power supply, PLUS is a straight-through positive output, and CONTROL is a second positive output interrupted by a switch.

Wire the motor leads to the COMMON and CONTROL terminals on the barrier strip. Connect one wire from PLUS to the COMMON (C)

A drivewheel and crank, mounted on a plate under the layout, control the wig-wag. The mechanism works like the drive rod on a steam locomotive.

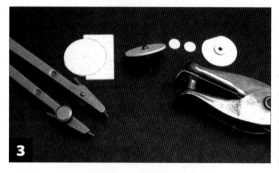

To make a cam, scribe a circle in styrene, snap it out, chuck it in a motor tool to round it, then punch out the hubs with a paper punch.

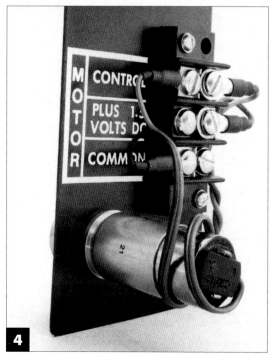

The reverse side of the mechanism plate shows the motor and the terminal strip. This keeps all wiring neat and makes mounting much easier.

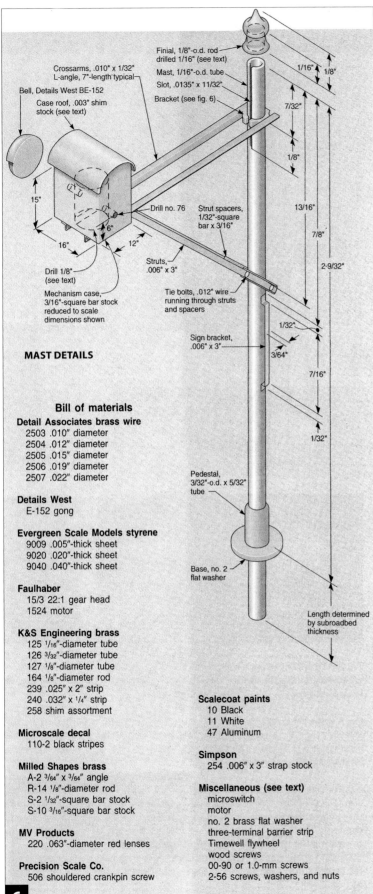

Crossarms, .010" x 1/32"
L-angle, 7"-length typical

Bell, Details West BE-152

Case roof, .003" shim stock (see text)

Finial, 1/8"-o.d. rod drilled 1/16" (see text)

Mast, 1/16"-o.d. tube

Slot, .0135" x 11/32"

Bracket (see fig. 6)

1/16" 1/8"

7/32"

1/8"

15"

6"

16" 12"

Drill no. 76

Strut spacers, 1/32"-square bar x 3/16"

13/16"

7/8"

2-9/32"

Drill 1/8" (see text)

Mechanism case, 3/16"-square bar stock reduced to scale dimensions shown

Struts, .006" x 3"

Tie bolts, .012" wire running through struts and spacers

1/32"

3/64"

Sign bracket, .006" x 3"

7/16"

1/32"

MAST DETAILS

Pedestal, 3/32"-o.d. x 5/32" tube

Length determined by subroadbed thickness

Base, no. 2 flat washer

Bill of materials

Detail Associates brass wire
2503 .010" diameter
2504 .012" diameter
2505 .015" diameter
2506 .019" diameter
2507 .022" diameter

Details West
E-152 gong

Evergreen Scale Models styrene
9009 .005"-thick sheet
9020 .020"-thick sheet
9040 .040"-thick sheet

Faulhaber
15/3 22:1 gear head
1524 motor

K&S Engineering brass
125 1/16"-diameter tube
126 3/32"-diameter tube
127 1/8"-diameter tube
164 1/8"-diameter rod
239 .025" x 2" strip
240 .032" x 1/4" strip
258 shim assortment

Microscale decal
110-2 black stripes

Milled Shapes brass
A-2 3/64" x 3/64" angle
R-14 1/8"-diameter rod
S-2 1/32"-square bar stock
S-10 3/16"-square bar stock

MV Products
220 .063"-diameter red lenses

Precision Scale Co.
506 shouldered crankpin screw

Scalecoat paints
10 Black
11 White
47 Aluminum

Simpson
254 .006" x 3" strap stock

Miscellaneous (see text)
microswitch
motor
no. 2 brass flat washer
three-terminal barrier strip
Timewell flywheel
wood screws
00-90 or 1.0-mm screws
2-56 screws, washers, and nuts

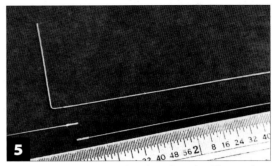

5

This view shows the completed motion wire. The portion hidden in the mast is .015" diameter and the visible portion is .012". The ends of each wire are filed flat to make a strong solder joint.

terminal on the microswitch and another wire from CONTROL to the normally open (NO) terminal.

Test the unit. The motor should run continuously with voltage applied to COMMON and CONTROL. Applying voltage to COMMON and PLUS should cause the motor to stop whenever the microswitch lever and flat spot on the cam coincide.

The drive mechanism

Add the drive wheel to the motor shaft. I used a Timewell No. 120 brass flywheel and drilled it to accept a crankpin screw, **1**. This crankpin is offset a scale 9" from the center of the flywheel's bore.

The brass connecting rod is drilled at one end to rotate freely on the crankpin screw shoulder. At the other end goes a brass retaining block. Drill the holes required in 3/16"-square bar stock before cutting this piece free and soldering it to the connecting rod.

Press the drive wheel onto the motor shaft with the crankpin screw opposite the cam's flat spot.

Make the baseplate and mount the motor bracket to it. My baseplate is a 3"-square piece of 1/8" Plexiglas. With the connecting rod full up or full down, drill a 3/32" hole in the baseplate directly above the retaining block hole. Make the shouldered sleeve bushing that will retain the signal mast, and align the motion wire.

Make the motion wire, **5**. For the sake of better appearance, I used lighter wire for the part of the motion wire that would be visible.

Building the signal

To figure the height of the signal mast, measure the distance from where the base of the mast will sit— usually at railhead level or slightly below—to the underside of the subroadbed. Mine was exactly 1". To this add the length of the retaining bushing (7/8") plus a scale 16'-6". Cut a section of 1/16" tube to that total length.

6

Cut an $^{11}/_{32}$"-long slot in one end of the mast tube, **6**. I used a Dremel No. 406 circular saw blade to cut a .010"-wide swath, which I widened to .0135" with a No. 80 drill bit in a motor tool. I pierced along the slot at intervals and carefully moved the bit back and forth like a milling cutter. These saw blades are no longer sold, but a No. 409 abrasive disk will work. Its .025" width won't look as good, but operation won't be affected.

Cut the two crossarms to length, **6**. Mine are 6 feet long. Prototypes ranged from four to seven feet depending on the situation.

My crossarms are Milled Shapes .010" x $^{1}/_{32}$" L-angle. This size (A-1) has been discontinued. The next smallest size is $^{3}/_{64}$" (A-2). You can also find similar stock from other makers. Next make the crossarm bracket, **7**, and solder the crossarms to it.

Make a mechanism case to the dimensions shown in **6**. It's easiest to file the roof contour and drill the holes before cutting the case off the end of your $^{3}/_{16}$"-square brass stock. To form the roof roll .003" shim stock between the shank of a $^{7}/_{32}$" drill and your fingertip. Solder the shim stock to the case, then use a sanding block, pulling down, to reduce the overhang to a scale inch all around.

Solder the mechanism case to the crossarms by pinning the components to a wood block, **8**. Unpin the assembly and slide the bracket down over the mast, adjusting it so that a scale 9" of slot extend below the crossarm bracket. Solder it to the mast.

Make the cantilever support struts, also shown in **6**. To make sure they're identical, bond them together with cyanoacrylate adhesive (CA) before drilling the holes. A little heat from your soldering iron will break them apart again, or you can soak them in acetone.

Solder the spacers to the struts and test-fit them. File the spacers until the struts come out parallel when positioned on the mast. Insert the pins that join the struts, then solder them and clip them off close to represent bolt heads. Make sure the struts are properly positioned, and solder them to the crossarms and mast.

Add the sign bracket and the pedestal. Position the base a scale 16'-6" from the top of the mast and solder. Turn the finial from brass rod. Test-fit but don't solder it to the mast, or it'll be in the way when you install the control rod.

For the bell, I modified a Details West gong casting by removing the bolt flange detail from around the perimeter and filing off the rear mounting stud. Then I cemented it to the case with epoxy.

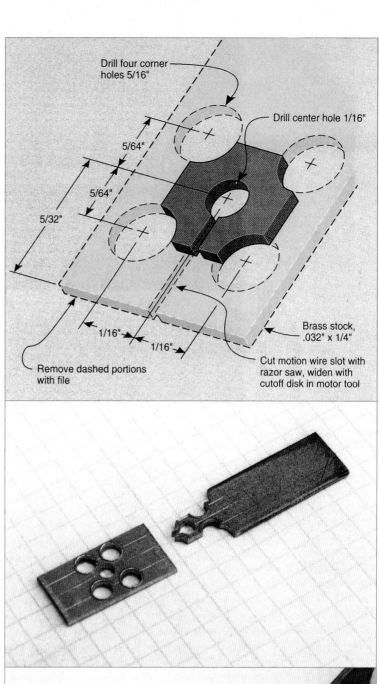

Drill four corner holes 5/16"

Drill center hole 1/16"

5/64"

5/64"

5/32"

1/16"

1/16"

Brass stock, .032" x 1/4"

Remove dashed portions with file

Cut motion wire slot with razor saw, widen with cutoff disk in motor tool

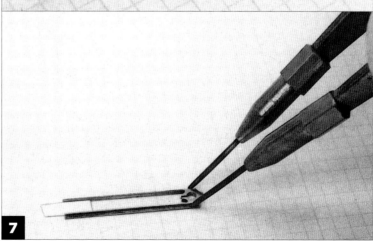

7

The crossarm bracket is made by drilling holes in brass and filing away everything that doesn't look like a bracket. The crossarms are soldered to the bracket with resistance-soldering tweezers. The graph paper helps with alignment.

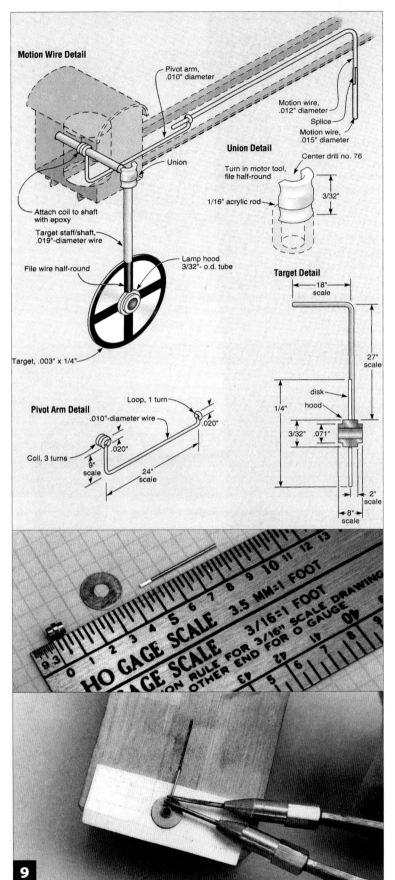

Motion Wire Detail

Pivot arm,
.010" diameter

Motion wire,
.012" diameter

Splice

Motion wire,
.015" diameter

Union

Union Detail

Center drill no. 76

Turn in motor tool,
file half-round

1/16" acrylic rod

3/32"

Attach coil to shaft
with epoxy

Target staff/shaft,
.019"-diameter wire

File wire half-round

Lamp hood
3/32"- o.d. tube

Target, .003" x 1/4"

Target Detail

18"
scale

27"
scale

disk
hood

1/4"

3/32" .071"

2"
scale

8"
scale

Pivot Arm Detail

Loop, 1 turn

.010"-diameter wire

.020"

.020"

Coil, 3 turns

9"
scale

24"
scale

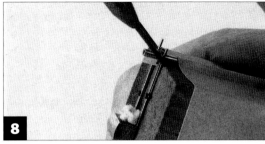

8

Wood blocks are handy for tacking down pieces as they are soldered.

Making the target

The parts that make up the target are shown in **9**. To make the flat disk I first used of dividers to impress a center hole in a piece of .003" shim brass. Then I lightly scribed a 1/4"-diameter circle. I enlarged the hole with a 3/32" bit, lined up the scribed circle with the hole in my paper punch, and stamped it out.

Next came the lens hood. I made mine by chucking a piece of 3/32" brass tube in my motor tool and turning the piece out with files.

To assemble the target I slid the finished hood onto a length of 1/16" tube and tacked it with a drop of CA. I worked the target disk onto the flange until it was centered and perpendicular, then I soldered it. Soaking the assembly in acetone dissolved the CA so I could remove the piece of 1/16" tube.

Next came the target shaft, filed flat on one end and soldered to the disk. Last came the union.

Painting

The parts are ready for painting, **10**. I etched the assemblies with aluminum oxide grit in a Paasche Air Eraser (small sandblaster) to provide "tooth" for paint adhesion. I masked off the horizontal portion of the target shaft with hookup wire insulation, as well as the vertical portion of the motion wire. Then I airbrushed all the parts with Scalecoat Aluminum, going back over the target and staff with white.

To mask off the 1"-wide black ring around the edge of the target, I used thin styrene circles, **11**. The cross stripes were added with decals and sealed with a clear finish.

Details and calibration

A 2"-long plug is needed to properly space the red lenses in the target hoods. I made mine by inserting 2" of a short length of 1/16" tube into a length of 3/32" tube and tacking with a drop of CA. Sand the exposed portion of the 1/16" tube on a disk sander until it's flush with the larger tube. Soak the parts in acetone, and extract the plug. Center the 2"-long

9

Here are the pieces used to make the target. A simple wood jig and graph paper help ensure the shaft is soldered in proper alignment with the disk.

plug inside the hood tube, then put in the lenses and secure them with Walthers Goo.

Form the pivot arm, **9**, then assemble the target shaft to the mechanism housing. Do this at the workbench—installation on the layout comes later.

Insert the motion wire into the mast and trim the horizontal leg so it clears the mechanism case. Check that the wire is parallel to the crossarms, bending it if necessary. Rotate the target to its extreme left position, and snip off the end of the motion wire just shy of the loop. Bend the motion wire enough to engage it in the loop.

Next, lower the signal mast into the baseplate bushing while feeding the .015" leg of the motion wire through the hole in the connecting-rod block. Lock the mast with the bushing set screw.

Turn the drive wheel so its crankpin is at either 3 or 9 o'clock, and snug down the connecting-rod block. Turning the drive wheel by hand, run the motion wire to its highest and lowest extremities. It should extend a scale 9" above and below the center of the crossarms. If not, loosen the set screw and adjust. Again turning the drive wheel, observe the target. It should describe equal arcs to the left and right. If it doesn't, bend the pivot arm slightly to adjust it.

Operate the signal under power to test the stopping action of the micro-switch. If the target doesn't come to rest straight down, adjust the relationship between the flat spot on the cam and the drive wheel crankpin by twisting the cam on the motor shaft.

Laminate the signs, **12**, to .005" styrene with spray adhesive, and fasten them to the mast bracket with five-minute epoxy.

Installation on the layout

Drill a No. 52 hole through the layout 13 feet from the near rail and sufficiently to the right of the roadway so the target doesn't swing out beyond the curb line. Remove the signal from the bushing, and substitute a short length of ¹⁄₁₆" tube protruding ¼" above the baseplate. Key this tube into the layout hole from underneath. Drill three starter holes for wood screws and secure the baseplate. Remove the ¹⁄₁₆" tube, and try inserting the signal from the top of the layout. If the mast binds, enlarge the subroadbed hole to ⁵⁄₆₄" or larger until the mast slips easily into the bushing.

Connect the barrier strip to your power source. I used a GRS CIL-125 LitePac controlled by a Circuitron DT-2 detection unit and ER-1 relay with the BR-2 bell ringer added for some sound effects.

Your model motormen and motorists will now be much safer.

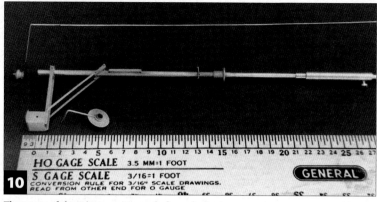

10

HO GAGE SCALE 3.5 MM=1 FOOT
S GAGE SCALE 3/16=1 FOOT
CONVERSION RULE FOR 3/16" SCALE DRAWINGS.
READ FROM OTHER END FOR O GAUGE **GENERAL**

The parts of the wig-wag are ready for painting.

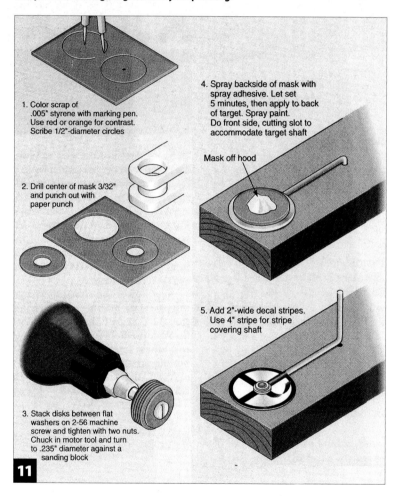

1. Color scrap of .005" styrene with marking pen. Use red or orange for contrast. Scribe 1/2"-diameter circles

2. Drill center of mask 3/32" and punch out with paper punch

3. Stack disks between flat washers on 2-56 machine screw and tighten with two nuts. Chuck in motor tool and turn to .235" diameter against a sanding block

4. Spray backside of mask with spray adhesive. Let set 5 minutes, then apply to back of target. Spray paint. Do front side, cutting slot to accommodate target shaft

Mask off hood

5. Add 2"-wide decal stripes. Use 4" stripe for stripe covering shaft

11

12

You can photocopy these signs and cut them out for use on your scale signal.

1

Photos by Gary Evans

3 How to animate overhead doors

By Steven Peck

Lehigh Valley No. 215 pulls into a shop stall for servicing as workers adjust a door in the adjacent stall. Steven motorized the doors, which can be operated from a panel mounted on the layout fascia.

Realism and functionality are things we strive for in model railroading. As I started building the engine and car shops for my layout, I thought it would be nice if there was a working transfer table and working building doors, **1**. Then I could incorporate the buildings into my operating sessions to improve realism.

With this setup, I used nylon cords for cables and a Torquemaster motor for a winch. An alternative to the Torquemaster is a Hankscraft 3440 1-rpm motor (www.hmimotors.com).

Buildings for the scene

My scene includes a Walthers car shop, back shop, and transfer table. I converted the three-stall car shop into one with six stalls by moving the back wall to the front. I then used ¼" plywood and styrene brick sheets to make a new back wall. This way, the only entrance to this structure is through the front of the building, **2**, **3**.

For the three-stall back shop, I used three Torquemaster motors. They operate the front and back doors simultaneously. I used six motors for the six-stall car

Parts list

Hankscraft Inc.

3440 1 rpm motor, 9

Wm. K. Walthers

Car shop

Engine shop

Miscellaneous

¼ oz. weight (for back of door)

¼" plywood

⅜" eyelets

⁵⁄₁₆"-square balsa

1" dowel

DPDT c/o toggle switches

No. 10 barrel swivel

Nylon cord

Snap swivel

Standard toggle switches

Styrene brick sheets

Throw arm

U-shaped stripwood

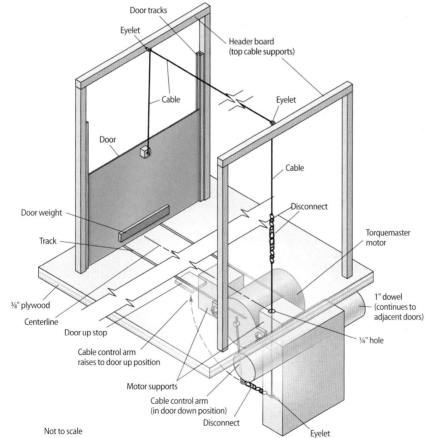

Door tracks

Eyelet

Header board (top cable supports)

Cable

Eyelet

Door

Cable

Door weight

Disconnect

Track

Torquemaster motor

⅜" plywood

Centerline

1" dowel (continues to adjacent doors)

Door up stop

¼" hole

Cable control arm raises to door up position

Motor supports

Cable control arm (in door down position)

Disconnect

Not to scale

Eyelet

2

This photo and diagram show how the cable is threaded for each of the six doors. Steven included disconnects for the cables in case he ever needs to re-string them or remove the building for cleaning.

This three-stall building allows locomotives to pass through it so they can get to the car shop. The doors across from each other are attached to a center cable, opening both doors simultaneously.

3

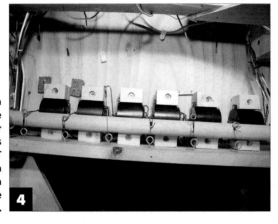

Motors for each car shop door are mounted under the layout. Each is wired to a DPDT center-off switch on a control panel, which is mounted to the layout's fascia.

4

The flat-blade toggle switches control the doors and have a center-off position so the doors can be stopped in any position. The rounded toggle switches control the power to the shop tracks.

5

shop. Tracks in both buildings connect with a transfer table, making it very much like a portion of the shops once used by the Lehigh Valley RR in Sayre, Pa.

Mounting the motors

As you can see in the door construction diagram, **2**, I marked the center line of the door and interior rails to align the various components of the door.

I mounted the motor horizontally so it's touching the underside of the benchwork. I made sure that the top of the rotating shaft and throw arm were in line with the ¼" hole that I drilled through the base plate. I then screwed a ⅜" eyelet in line with this hole, making sure it was level with the throw arm

in the down position. I placed a 1" dowel parallel to the motor as a stop and cable guide.

Setting up the door components

I made two U-shaped tracks for the door from stripwood (styrene U channel would also work) and glued them inside the door openings. I painted them concrete gray and placed the doors in the tracks. I made sure the doors had clearance to slide easily.

I attached pieces of ⁵⁄₁₆"-square balsa to the front and back walls for an eyelet header board, and placed them high enough so the doors had room to open. I installed ⅜" eyelets on the center line of each of the header boards. The eyelets guide the cable to the motor mechanism.

Running the cable

After I tied each cable to the door eyelet, I ran it up through the eyelet above the door, across the shop interior, and down through the back eyelet. I tied a No. 10 barrel swivel to the cable about a quarter of the way down the back wall with the door in the down position.

I tied a snap swivel to a 1" piece of cable and dropped it down the ¼" hole to the motor. I then connected the snap swivel to the barrel swivel. This is an easy disconnect for the cable in case there is a need to re-cable or to remove the building for cleaning, **2**.

With the motor throw arm in the down position, I tied the cable to a snap swivel and connected it to the throw arm. It just needs a little slack to allow the door to go down all the way.

To determine the full open position of the door, I moved the throw arm to the up position by hand. I removed any slack in the cable and found that the final tension can be adjusted by wrapping it around the door eyelet or by bending the control arm slightly. I also used a resistor on the motor to open and close the doors at a realistically slow speed.

Operating the doors

I mounted the motors under the benchwork, **4**. They're controlled by double-pole double-throw (DPDT) center-off toggle switches. The control panel, **5**, is a basic map of the car shop, transfer table, and engine shop. The flat blade switches are for the doors and have a center off-position that allows me to stop the doors in any position. I used standard toggles for the track blocks.

You can apply this type of mechanism to any rail-served industry. It's an easy project to complete and is a great way to add realism to your layout.

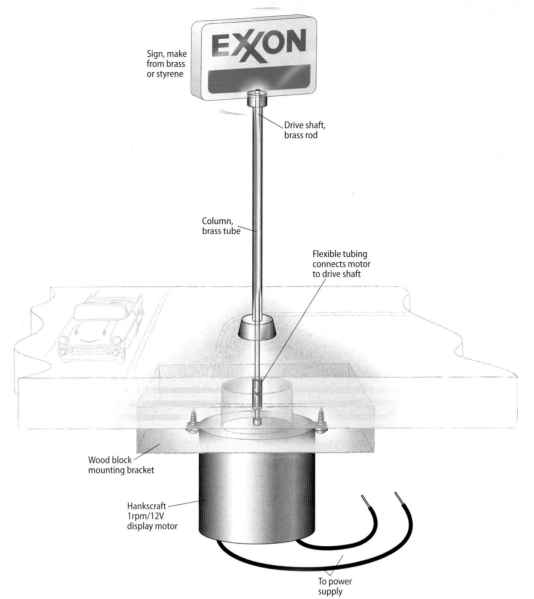

Sign, make from brass or styrene

Drive shaft, brass rod

Column, brass tube

Flexible tubing connects motor to drive shaft

Wood block mounting bracket

Hankscraft 1rpm/12V display motor

To power supply

Simple rotating signs 4

By David Popp

An American icon of the mid-20th century is the rotating service-station sign. In marketing, anything that catches the consumer's eye has potential to sell a product, and moving signs were good at it. Growing up in the '60s and '70s, I remember seeing a number of rotating gas station signs around town, including Clark, Standard, and my uncle's Union 76 station.

Bill Day, of Potomac Falls, Va., sent us this idea for making your own rotating service station sign. The key component for this project is a low-rpm display motor. (We've shown a Hankscraft 1-rpm

switch motor here). The shaft for the sign is made from two pieces of brass. A length of brass tubing serves as the mast, and a piece of rod with a diameter small enough to fit inside the mast drives the sign. The sign itself can be sheet brass or styrene.

The motor is mounted under the layout. To connect the motor shaft to the drive rod, Bill used a small piece of vinyl tubing that fit snugly over both the rod and shaft, though you could use a brass sleeve with set screws instead. Almost any 12-volt power supply will work for the motor.

Rotating signs were used by service stations as well as restaurants and other businesses. Old oil-company road maps are a great source of graphics. You can also make your own artwork, print it out, and mount it to the sign face.

WAHSATCH TUNNEL
LENGTH 8 MILES   ELEV 6247
COMPLETED 1929

Photos by the author

5 Build an operating tunnel curtain

By Gary Hoover

With the tunnel curtain up, a Missouri, Kansas & Quincy train emerges from the portal.

If you're looking for a way to add animation to a tunnel scene, borrow a practice used by the Burlington Northern Santa Fe. I've visited the former Great Northern line at Stevens Pass, cut through the rugged, beautiful Cascade mountains of northern Washington. There, the eight-mile-long Cascade Tunnel features a forced-air ventilation system that prevents train crews from being asphyxiated by exhaust.

Powerful blowers on the east end of the tunnel draw in fresh air and force it out the west portal. To keep the fresh air flowing properly through the tunnel, a metal "curtain" is used to close the eastern end while the blowers are operating.

When a train approaches from either direction, the tunnel curtain rises, much like an automatic garage door, accompanied by a whoosh of air into the tunnel. After the train clears the tunnel, the curtain closes.

After seeing this dramatic operation in real life, I quickly decided that my HO scale Missouri, Kansas & Quincy needed a similar tunnel curtain for its Wahsatch Tunnel, **1**. I spent the entire plane ride back home from Washington sketching the prelimi-

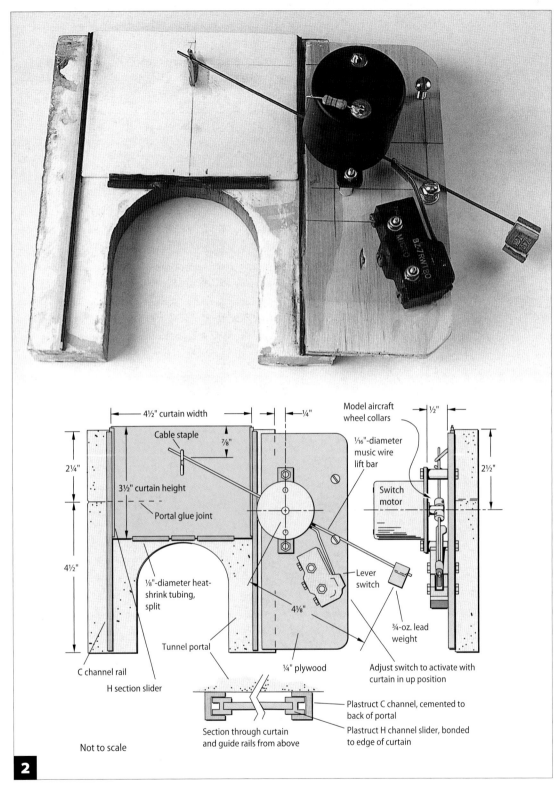

2

4½" curtain width — ¼"

Cable staple

7/8"

2¼"

3½" curtain height

Portal glue joint

4½"

⅛"-diameter heat-shrink tubing, split

Tunnel portal

C channel rail

H section slider

Not to scale

Model aircraft wheel collars

1/16"-diameter music wire lift bar

½"

Switch motor

2½"

4⅛"

Lever switch

¼" plywood

¾-oz. lead weight

Adjust switch to activate with curtain in up position

Section through curtain and guide rails from above

Plastruct C channel, cemented to back of portal

Plastruct H channel slider, bonded to edge of curtain

A slow-motion switch motor raises the curtain at a realistic speed. The photo and illustration show how I built and installed the curtain and other coponents.

nary design for my operating HO scale version. I couldn't wait to get started!

I wanted my operating door to be absolutely reliable. The embarrassing thought of a train crashing through a stuck tunnel curtain during an open house passed through my mind more than once. A simple fail-safe electrical circuit keeps this from happening.

I also wanted automatic operation. The MKQ uses the Circuitron optical-detection system for its automatic signal system, so I used it also to detect trains approaching the tunnel and to open the curtain.

Finally, I wanted the MKQ's operating curtain to capture the drama and flavor of the real Cascade Tunnel, although I didn't try modeling an exact scale replica. Since mine is a free-lance railroad, I could do that without inviting a nitpicker attack.

Draw the curtain

The dimensions and locations of the parts for HO scale are shown in **2**. I had to cut and glue the portals to obtain the height needed when the curtain is in the up position, **3**.

Cut the plaster portal with a sharp, wide razor saw. Work slowly and clean the blade often. A very light coat of Pam vegetable spray on the blade helps.

I joined the two portal halves with epoxy and let them dry on a flat, hard surface. The portal front and sides can be painted using your favorite technique. Don't paint the back of the portal because you'll need a good gluing surface for components.

I used Evergreen V-groove scribed styrene siding for the curtain, cutting the width first. For the curtain to operate smoothly, it must have a constant width. The curtain was initially cut about twice as long as it would finally be. This helps align the rails when they're bonded to the portal. I bonded a strip of Plastruct H section to each edge of the curtain to get a smooth sliding fit between the curtain and the rails. The H section rides inside the C-channel rails glued to the portal.

To engage the lift bar, I glued a wire-cable staple (brad) to the rear of the curtain with epoxy. A piece of brass strip could serve the same purpose.

Finally, I slit three short segments of heat-shrink tubing and cemented them to the bottom of the curtain for a soft cushion air seal. Paint and decal stripes finished this stage.

Another kind of rail

The portal rails must be straight, spaced properly, and free of glue, paint, and nicks. The first step in installing the rails was aligning the tunnel portal with the center line of the curtain or vice versa.

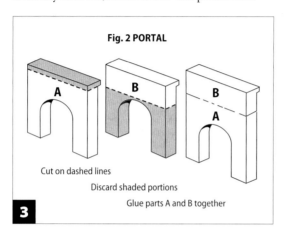

Fig. 2 PORTAL

A

B

B

A

Cut on dashed lines

Discard shaded portions

Glue parts A and B together

3

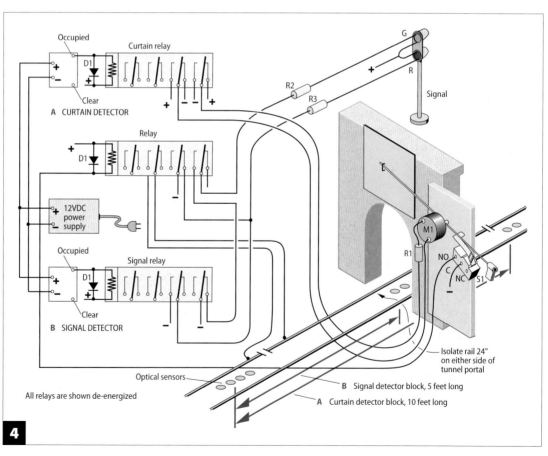

Occupied

Curtain relay

D1

Clear

A CURTAIN DETECTOR

Relay

D1

12VDC power supply

Occupied

Signal relay

D1

Clear

B SIGNAL DETECTOR

Optical sensors

All relays are shown de-energized

G

R2

R3

+

R

Signal

M1

R1

NO

C

NC

S1

Isolate rail 24" on either side of tunnel portal

B Signal detector block, 5 feet long

A Curtain detector block, 10 feet long

4

Bill of Materials

A. I. M.	Plastruct
126 abutment wings, 2	C-4 C channel, ⅛" x .050"
128 poured concrete tunnel portal, 2	**Radio Shack**
A-Line	(D1) 275-214A relay, 12VDC, 3
13000 lead weight (.75 oz.)	(D1) 276-1144 diode, 3
Badger	(R1) 271-153A resistor, 1,000 ohm
16107 Accu-Flex gloss white paint	(S1) 275-016 lever switch
Circuitron	(S1) 278-1215 22-gauge wire
5501 BD-1 block detector, 2	**Switchmaster**
Con-Cor	(M1) 169J1001 switch motor
222-9060 power substation	**Wm. K. Walthers**
Du-Bro	934-703084 decal stripes, red
596 ³⁄₃₂" aircraft wheel collars, 2	**Miscellaneous**
Evergreen	¼" x 3" x 7" plywood
14250 V-groove siding	⅛"-diameter shrink tube
Great Glass	¹⁄₁₆"-diameter music wire
15009 Kelly green glass stain (for insulators)	mounting hardware
Oregon Rail Supply	solder
114 two-light signal (includes LED and resistors R2 and R3)	wire-cable brad or brass strip

5

Here's the completed curtain in its closed position. The main walls of the blower house are AIM Products tapered abutment wings, with the remainder of the structure cobbled together from various leftover kit parts I had in my scrapbox. The power station is a Con-Cor kit.

Next, I set the C-channel portal rails in place with a very slight gap remaining between them and the curtain edges. Finally, when everything was aligned, I tack-glued the top and bottom of each rail with a drop of cyanoacrylate adhesive (CA).

I gently slid the curtain up and down by hand to make sure everything was working correctly. It should travel up and down the track smoothly and by its own weight. If it doesn't, something is binding. For a finishing touch, I added a fillet of epoxy along the entire outer edge of each portal rail. As the epoxy set, I continued to check the curtain for proper operation.

Get the motor running

I mounted the slow-moving Switchmaster switch motor to a piece of ¼" plywood that I epoxied to the back side of the portal. I added .75 ounces of lead to the free end of the throw bar to help balance the curtain's weight. Without it, the curtain traveled too fast going down and too slow going up. Next, I tested the motor to make sure everything worked properly. The remainder of the structure is shown in **5**.

The fail-safe device

The electrical system is shown in **4**. I used two Circuitron optical-detector blocks: One triggers the tunnel-curtain operation and the other triggers the signal at the portal. The signal-detection block overlaps the tunnel-curtain detection block.

The two-aspect signal is red when the curtain is down and will only display green if the curtain is fully up and no other trains are in the signal-detection block. This interlocking feature between was easily accomplished by routing the power through relays.

The fail-safe feature uses the position of the curtain to control power to a short section of rail on either side of the portal. When the curtain is up, a small lever switch closes and provides power to the track. If the curtain fails to open completely, the locomotive will stop on the dead section of track before it hits the curtain.

I used a resistor with the Switchmaster motor for realistic curtain operating speed. You may need to vary the resistor value for your particular application.

The real fun with the tunnel curtain lies in its operation. I especially enjoy watching first-time visitors when they spot the closed tunnel curtain with a train approaching. To their amazement, the curtain slowly rises just before the train arrives. At the same time, the red signal winks to green. It's a bit of fun that never gets old.

Photos by Cody Grivno

6 Moving vehicles for your HO or N layout

By Terry Thompson

A city bus and other moving traffic adds interest to downtown Neustadt on Terry Thompson's HO scale German layout. The vehicles follow two different routes as they travel through the central business district.

Hands down, the most attention-getting item on my new German prototype layout isn't a locomotive, freight car, or structure. It's a bus. Not just any bus, however, but a motorized HO scale city bus that travels a route through the town, makes stops for passengers, and obeys traffic signals.

The bus (and the truck that shares the streets with it) is made by Faller. In the United States, Faller is best known for its structure kits, but the company's Faller Car System, available in HO and N scales, is popular in Europe.

Faller's basic system uses a steel wire embedded in the road to guide the vehicles. Each vehicle has a rechargeable battery, can motor, steerable front axle that follows the wire via magnets, and a conventional on-off switch and a reed switch. You can place devices in the road that will stop the cars momentarily, stop them until you release them (Faller refers to this as "parking"), or cause them to change routes.

I'll guide you through the basics of the system and take you step-by-step through the techniques required to get the system up and running on a layout.

2

STARTER KIT. The easiest way to begin is by purchasing one of the starter sets that include a powered vehicle, steel guide wire, recharger, and plaster for the road. The vehicle choices range from cars and buses to trucks and tractors. Faller changes the vehicle selections frequently, so you have many options.

3

VEHICLE CHASSIS. Each vehicle has steerable front wheels and a powered rear axle. The worm drive is very quiet, but makes for abrupt stops. That's important for the system, however, because the vehicles must stop over control sections, not coast beyond them. Note also the reed switch and the added magnet.

4

STEEL WIRE, CUTTER. You'll need a suitable hard wire cutter, like this Xuron No. 90033, to trim the wire. Paint the wire with a lacquer-based paint prior to installation, otherwise moisture from your scenery can cause the wire to rust and stain the road.

5

CITY PLANNING. My first step was to map out the route showing specific structure locations and noting the placement of any buried controls. Remember, you're dealing with close clearances and tight curves here, just as if you were planning a model railroad. The bus has especially long overhangs, so I had to allow for those. Also mark any one-way streets.

6

TEST RUNS. I put the guide wire in place using transparent tape and test-ran the vehicles. At this point I couldn't test the control system, but I could run the vehicles around the system to check the corner clearances on the various curves.

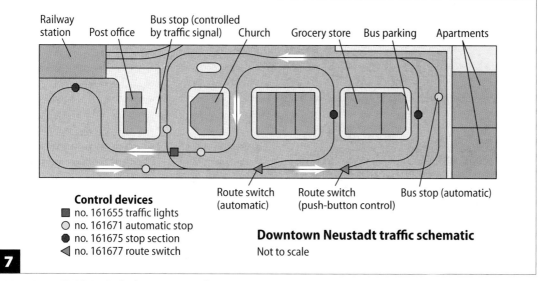

7

Railway station · Post office · Bus stop (controlled by traffic signal) · Church · Grocery store · Bus parking · Apartments

Control devices
- ■ no. 161655 traffic lights
- ○ no. 161671 automatic stop
- ● no. 161675 stop section
- ◁ no. 161677 route switch

Route switch (automatic) · Route switch (push-button control) · Bus stop (automatic)

Downtown Neustadt traffic schematic
Not to scale

BUS AND TRUCK ROUTES. The bus route runs from a stop near the railroad station to the other end of town. A control in the roadway can divert the bus into a parking section if I want to stop the operation. On the second route, a delivery truck goes from the station to the grocery store and back. At both locations, parking sections keep the truck in place until I release it. The truck and bus use the same guide wire for several feet but otherwise travel on different routes. A traffic light with stop sections buried in the roads keeps the two vehicles from colliding at the intersection.

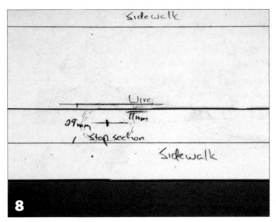

8

LOCATING THE GUIDE WIRE. Next, I carefully marked the location of the guide wire and all of the controllers using the Faller templates. The magnetic field created by the controllers is tightly focused, so their positioning is critical. I had to relocate one that I placed on a curve.

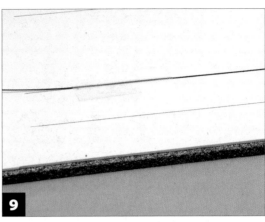

9

PAVEMENT. I paved my streets with a layer of .080" styrene on top of ¼" sheet cork that rests on the plywood subroadbed. Two other options that I could have chosen were using Faller streets (this would have been easier, but I wanted to create my own curves) or plaster (easier to carve but once you pour it, you can't move it).

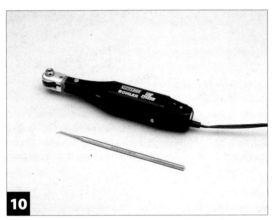

10

CUTTING THE GROOVE. I tried several approaches for carving the groove for the wire, including several different bits in a motor tool. My best results came with the Faller motorized cutter and a scriber from Bare Metal Foil. Both worked well, though the power tool was faster. I also used files to touch up the grooves.

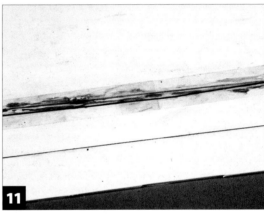

11

CHECKING THE GUIDE WIRE. Once the grooves were in the streets, I temporarily taped the wires in place for testing. I found that a few adjustments were still needed. It was a simple task to fill the problem grooves and make new ones. I left the pieces of wire a little bit long so I could make small adjustments before doing a final trim.

12

SPECIAL CONTROLS. The controls require a 1¹⁄₁₆" hole at the center of each location. An adjustable bit cuts the large circle in the road and cork. Next, I reset the bit to match the Faller templates and drilled halfway through the plywood from each side to make a clean hole. Finally, I used a chisel to cut notches for the mounting brackets.

13

SECURING THE WIRE. With the control devices in place, I tested the system one more time, energizing the devices as needed. Then I trimmed the wire to size, cleaned it with solvent, and applied a coat of Krylon clear spray. Once the clear coat was dry, I installed the wire with cyanoacrylate adhesive (CA) and bits of tape.

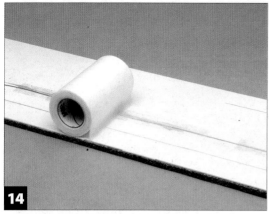

14 SURFACING THE PAVEMENT. I covered the guide wire and styrene pavement with 3" wide paper surgical adhesive tape. This tape's surface is rough enough to give the vehicles some traction, but not so sticky that it interferes with the guide magnet. (My original plan was to use self-adhesive foam streets, but they had too much grip.)

15 BRICK PAVEMENT. For the town square I covered the styrene and wire with vacuum-formed brick sheet from The N Scale Architect. The .020" thick sheet doesn't interfere with the guide magnet's attraction to the wire. I shimmed each joint in the pavement so the road surface stepped down slightly at each asphalt-brick transition to keep the guide magnets from catching.

16 PAINTING THE PAVEMENT. Using an airbrush and Faller's roadway paint, thinned with Tamiya X-20 thinner, I spray-painted the asphalt. The tape absorbs a lot of paint. Don't put too much paint on at once or you'll weaken the bond between the tape and the styrene. I painted the brick gray and then dry-brushed it with brick red.

17 WEATHERING THE ROADWAY. Again using an airbrush, I added some black streaks to the pavement to simulate the surface weathering produced by the passing traffic. The streaks are darker in the lanes that carry the heaviest traffic. Adding some variations with medium gray helps break up the monotony of the pavement color.

18 ROAD MARKINGS. Dry-transfer road markings, striping, and lettering are made by Faller and others. I looked at German streets on Google Earth to get the general idea. Are all my layout's roadway markings correct? Probably not, but most of the Faller markings cover functions similar to those in the U.S., so they seem plausible.

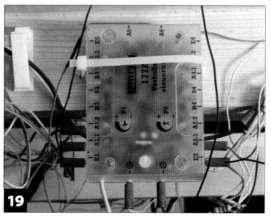

19 CONTROL LOCATIONS. The system's sensors, timers, and solenoids get power from a small Märklin power pack. Some of my Faller controllers receive signals from the sensors in the road to activate the stop sections. I mounted the control boxes on the side of an L girder under the layout.

Photos by the author

7 Build an operating windmill

By Rodger Gredvig

Providing motion to an otherwise static scene, the author's scratchbuilt windmill appears to be pumping water for an adjacent railroad water tank.

I discovered a simple way to use an aquarium pump motor to make a spinning windmill, suitable for even N scale's small size.

The drawings show most of the story. For my first attempt I used parts from the Campbell HO windmill kit, No. 1604. I built a new tower from Plastruct A-3 ³⁄₃₂" angles, with .030"-square styrene strip for the diagonal bracing.

I filed down the cast ring located about midway out on the fan blades to reduce its bulk. I filed down the drive shaft to allow free movement of the fan,

and I also cut down the size of the vane. Position the fan on the drive shaft, and carefully form a small mushroom-shaped cap on the shaft end with a soldering iron. Make certain that the fan spins freely.

I made a smaller version suitable for N scale from spoked sequins. I trimmed two sequins to make them a scale 8'-0" in diameter and separated them with a wire ring, with the blades staggered. The ring was made by wrapping 24-gauge copper wire around a AAA battery. Because of its light mass this model doesn't operate as smoothly as the Campbell one.

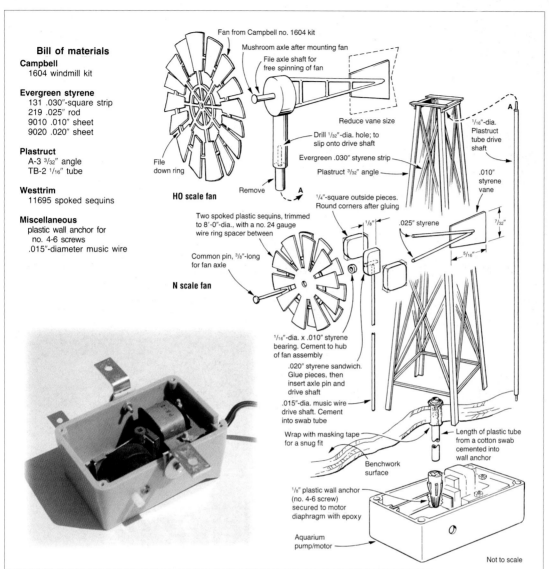

Bill of materials

Campbell
1604 windmill kit

Evergreen styrene
131 .030"-square strip
219 .025" rod
9010 .010" sheet
9020 .020" sheet

Plastruct
A-3 3/32" angle
TB-2 1/16" tube

Westtrim
11695 spoked sequins

Miscellaneous
plastic wall anchor for
no. 4-6 screws
.015"-diameter music wire

Fan from Campbell no. 1604 kit

Mushroom axle after mounting fan

File axle shaft for free spinning of fan

Reduce vane size

Drill 1/32"-dia. hole; to slip onto drive shaft

Evergreen .030" styrene strip

Plastruct 3/32" angle

File down ring

Remove

HO scale fan

1/16"-dia. Plastruct tube drive shaft

.010" styrene vane

1/4"-square outside pieces. Round corners after gluing

Two spoked plastic sequins, trimmed to 8'-0"-dia., with a no. 24 gauge wire ring spacer between

1/8"

.025" styrene

7/32"

5/16"

Common pin, 3/8"-long for fan axle

N scale fan

1/16"-dia. x .010" styrene bearing. Cement to hub of fan assembly

.020" styrene sandwich. Glue pieces, then insert axle pin and drive shaft

.015"-dia. music wire drive shaft. Cement into swab tube

Wrap with masking tape for a snug fit

Benchwork surface

Length of plastic tube from a cotton swab cemented into wall anchor

1/8" plastic wall anchor (no. 4-6 screw) secured to motor diaphragm with epoxy

Aquarium pump/motor

Not to scale

The inset photo shows the aquarium pump ready for mounting under the layout. The drawings show the construction. Make sure the blades rotate freely on the shaft. Paint the completed windmill dull silver and weather it appropriately.

For the fan shaft, I used a straight pin cemented into a simulated gearbox housing (made with layers of .020" styrene that were cut and filed to shape). The construction of the gearbox and the directional vane is shown above. Fashion and cement a .062"-diameter circle of .010" styrene to the fan as a bearing hub.

Vibration will cause the fan to spin, so I made a drive system using an aquarium pump. Cut a length of plastic tube from a cotton swab (or similar material) and wrap a few turns of masking tape around it. Drill a hole in the layout base to provide a snug fit around the tape. Attach a small plastic wall anchor to the pump diaphragm with epoxy. The pump is mounted under the layout with wood screws, separated from the wood by rubber grommets to reduce vibration, and centered under the hole.

The drive shaft to the fan assembly is 1/16" Plastruct tube with a wire center with the top end trimmed as shown above and cemented into the fan gear housing.

Press-fit it into the small wall anchor at the bottom. Drill out the platform opening at the top of the tower to 3/16" diameter. The drive shaft must not touch the tower structure, or it will shake the tower to pieces.

The windmill must also point in certain directions, determined by experimentation, to get the proper harmonics to make the fan spin. Otherwise you'll get a lot of chattering, and the assembly will vibrate without the fan rotating.

I wired a 110-volt dimmer switch into the pump line to slow the pump motor, smooth out the oscillation, and reduce chattering.

WARNING: Readers unfamiliar with electrical safety precautions should not make the 110-volt connections. These must be made properly to avoid the possibility of a dangerous, potentially fatal electric shock.

The finished windmill is certain to attract attention from visitors as well as regular operators.

8 Build a working track scale

By Jim Ferenc

Author Jim Ferenc's son tallies the weights of loaded hopper cars as the locomotive moves cars into position on the working track scale on Jim's HO Colorado & Southern layout.

On my HO scale Colorado & Southern Ry., the mines around Louisville, Colo., share a track scale that weighs the cars and displays their weight in gross tons, adding a novel and realistic flair to operations.

Like many older real scales, my modeled scale track is separate from the siding track and shifted over about a foot in a gantlet, **1**, done to keep the locomotive's weight off of the scale. As the engine travels on the siding, the cars are switched to the scale track through "frogless" turnouts.

My model scale uses vertical movement (less than a scale 6") to drive an electronic meter displaying the car's weight in tons. An empty hopper weighing two real ounces will display a gross weight of about 20 tons (its "tare"). I use crushed and sifted real coal, so a loaded two-bay car weighs four ounces, which shows as a gross weight of about 75 tons.

How it works

The track scale has three major assemblies: the scale mechanism, the circuit board, and the track, **2**.

The author built his scale on a curve, but recommends building one on straight track if possible.

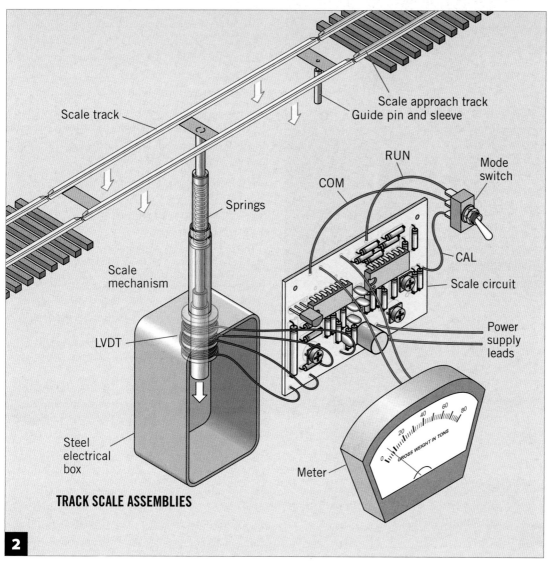

Scale track

Scale approach track
Guide pin and sleeve

RUN

Mode switch

COM

Springs

CAL

Scale mechanism

Scale circuit

LVDT

Power supply leads

Steel electrical box

Meter

GROSS WEIGHT IN TONS

TRACK SCALE ASSEMBLIES

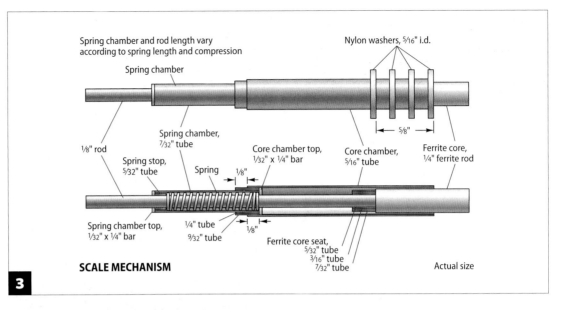

Spring chamber and rod length vary according to spring length and compression

Nylon washers, 5/16" i.d.

Spring chamber

5/8"

1/8" rod

Spring chamber, 7/32" tube

Spring stop, 5/32" tube

Spring

Core chamber top, 1/32" x 1/4" bar

Core chamber, 5/16" tube

Ferrite core, 1/4" ferrite rod

1/8"

Spring chamber top, 1/32" x 1/4" bar

1/4" tube

9/32" tube

1/8"

Ferrite core seat, 5/32" tube 3/16" tube 7/32" tube

Actual size

SCALE MECHANISM

3

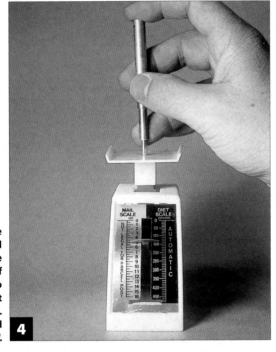

Press down on the mechanism until the scale shows the maximum weight of the cars you intend to weigh, plus the weight of the mechanism. The spring should compress a scale 6".

4

Cut

Cut

Spring 1

Spring 2

Screw the coils of spring 2 into the coils of spring 1

COMBINING SPRINGS

5

The mechanism is the brass equivalent of a retractable ballpoint pen. The only support for the scale track is the mechanism rod, although there is a guide pin at one end to keep it aligned.

The heart of the scale is a Linear Variable Displacement Transformer (LVDT), a transformer with a vertically movable core. Movement of the rod/core causes the LVDT to pass more or less signal from its primary windings to its secondary windings. The difference in signal strength is detected by the circuit. Cars that weigh less than two ounces will display 0 to 20 tons and heavier cars display 60 to 80 tons.

The parts list on page 40 shows what's needed. Parts that don't have a supplier listed can be bought at a hardware store. The springs came from two click-type ballpoint pens.

The only unusual component is the ferrite rod, used for the LVDT core. I listed Amidon Corporation as a source, but electronic surplus or supply shops may also have 1/4" rod. The rod needs to be about 1" long. To shorten a longer rod, score it with a knife and snap.

Mechanism

Build the mechanism as in **3**, starting with the core chamber. Be sure the hole in the chamber top is centered and easily clears a 1/8" brass rod. Slide the end of some 9/32" tubing into the chamber and use it to ensure the core chamber top is square with the walls of the chamber, about 1/8" in from the end of the 5/16" tube. Add flux and solder the top in place.

Nest the 7/32" spring chamber in the 1/4" and 9/32" rings. Flux and assemble, with the bottom of the spring chamber flush against the core chamber top.

Solder this assembly, working quickly to avoid un-soldering the core chamber top. Wipe with a damp cloth while everything is still hot for a clean joint.

Solder the ⁵⁄₃₂" spring stop about 2¾" from one end of a 4" length of ⅛" brass rod. Slide the pen spring onto the 2¾" end of the rod.

Your spring might have a different tension than mine, so you'll have to cut the ⅛" rod and spring chamber to match. Trim the top of the spring chamber flush with the top of the ⁵⁄₃₂" spring stop when the spring is uncompressed. Likewise, trim the bottom of the rod to be ⅝" inside the core chamber with the spring uncompressed.

Make the spring chamber top from ¹⁄₃₂" x ¼" brass bar with a hole that easily clears the ⅛" brass rod. Cut and file it to fit the top of the spring chamber. Assemble the rod with the spring inside the chamber assembly and slide the spring chamber top into place. Use masking tape to hold the spring chamber top in place. Mark the ⅛" rod a scale 6" above the spring chamber top.

Check the spring performance, **4**. A single pen spring compressed about a scale 10" for a four-ounce hopper. To stiffen this spring, I added a second spring, **5**.

Finishing the mechanism

Measure the distance from the top of the ⁵⁄₃₂" spring stop to the top of the ⅛" rod. Unsolder the spring stop and remove it and the spring from the ⅛" rod. Build a seat for gluing the ferrite core to the end of the rod, **3**.

Insert the ⅛" rod up through the two-chamber assembly as far as it will go. Slide the spring onto the rod. Reposition the ⁵⁄₃₂" spring stop and compress and clamp the spring out of the way. Flux and solder the spring stop in place. Put the spring chamber top in place a final time. Look into the core chamber to ensure the rod is in the middle of the chamber, adjusting the spring chamber top if necessary. Solder the spring chamber top in place. Gently file any solder blobs to make the spring chamber outer wall smooth. Cut the ⅛" rod so that at least a scale 9" of the rod will be above your roadbed.

Adding the LVDT

Use cyanoacrylate adhesive (CA) to glue a ⁵⁄₁₆" nylon washer with its bottom edge ⅝" above the bottom of the core chamber. Slide two more washers onto the core chamber, then glue the final washer flush with the open end. Slide the middle washers to make three sections of equal size. Wrap each section

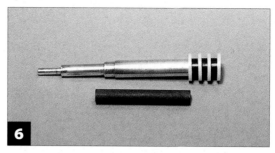

6

The scale mechanism is ready for winding with magnet wire. The ferrite rod is in the foreground.

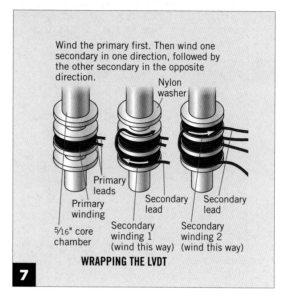

Wind the primary first. Then wind one secondary in one direction, followed by the other secondary in the opposite direction.

Nylon washer

Primary leads

Primary winding

⁵⁄₁₆" core chamber

Secondary lead

Secondary winding 1 (wind this way)

Secondary lead

Secondary winding 2 (wind this way)

WRAPPING THE LVDT

7

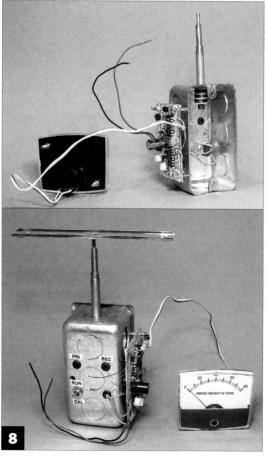

8

The mechanism is complete. This shows how the circuit board is mounted to the electrical box. Label all of the wires.

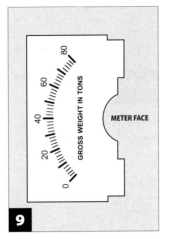

METER FACE

GROSS WEIGHT IN TONS

9

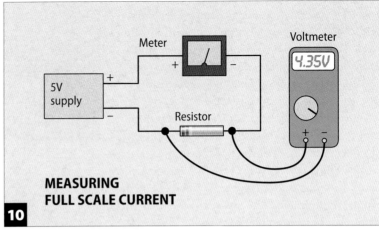

Meter

Voltmeter

4.35V

5V supply

Resistor

MEASURING FULL SCALE CURRENT

10

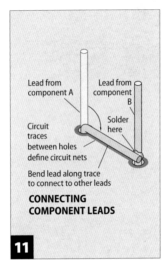

Lead from component A

Lead from component B

Circuit traces between holes define circuit nets

Solder here

Bend lead along trace to connect to other leads

CONNECTING COMPONENT LEADS

11

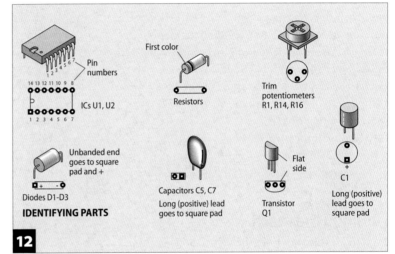

Pin numbers

ICs U1, U2

First color

Resistors

Trim potentiometers R1, R14, R16

Unbanded end goes to square pad and +

Diodes D1-D3

Capacitors C5, C7

Long (positive) lead goes to square pad

Transistor Q1

Flat side

C1

Long (positive) lead goes to square pad

IDENTIFYING PARTS

12

with a strip of electrical tape, cut to fit between the washers, **6**.

Wrap magnet wire around the core chamber, **7**. Leave an extra 9" of wire for each lead. Wrap the primary (center) section first with as many turns as possible between the washers. Wrap the secondary sections with one continuous strand. You must wrap the secondaries in opposite directions as shown—clockwise for one, counterclockwise for the other. Count the turns to ensure an equal number in each secondary. A drop of CA keeps them in place.

Use epoxy to glue the ferrite core to its seat at the end of the ⅛" rod. Avoid gluing the core to the chamber wall.

The LVDT is enclosed in a steel electrical box, **8**, which shields it from electrical interference. Drill a ⁵⁄₁₆" hole in the center of the top of the box for the mechanism. Drill holes for the mode switch and for the grommets for the LVDT wires. Drill three additional ⅛" holes for the screws that attach the circuit board to the side of the box. Use the circuit board layout on page 38 as a guide. The trace side of the board mounts toward the box.

Pass the scale mechanism, rod first, through the ⁵⁄₁₆" hole. Secure the mechanism to the box with CA on the top nylon washer of the LVDT. Route the LVDT primary and secondary wires through grommeted holes and be sure to label everything.

Scale electronics

The circuit schematic is shown on page 39, but you don't need to understand it to build it. The circuit parts list is on page 40. The meter, switch, and perfboard are available from Radio Shack. The other parts are available from Digi-Key and other suppliers. You'll need a 5V, 250mA power supply.

The meter face, **9**, is sized for the Radio Shack meter. Cut it out and glue it over the Radio Shack label with white glue. If you use the Radio Shack meter, skip ahead to the circuit board section.

If you use a different meter, you'll need to calculate a new value for R26. To do this, calculate the meter's full scale current (FSC). If you know the FSC, skip to step 3. Otherwise do the following:

1. Measure the FSC with the circuit in fig. 10. Start with a 100kΩ ¼W resistor (or a 100KΩ

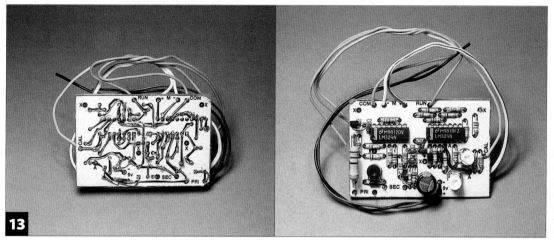

13

Simply tape the circuit diagrams to the perfboard. Note how component leads are soldered together on the trace side of the board.

potentiometer), and substitute smaller resistors until the meter's needle deflects to its maximum value.

2. Divide the voltage reading across the resistor by the resistor's value in ohms to get FSC in amps.

3. Divide 3.3 by the FSC (in amps) to get the value of R26 in ohms. For example, the Radio Shack meter has a 1 milliamp (.001A) full scale current. This leads to 3.3/.001 = 3300 or 3.3KΩ.

Circuit board and assembly basics

I mounted the electronic components on perfboard following the circuit layout on page 38.

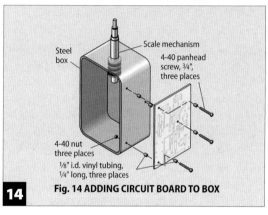

14

Steel box

Scale mechanism

4-40 panhead screw, ¾", three places

4-40 nut three places

⅛" i.d. vinyl tubing, ¼" long, three places

Fig. 14 ADDING CIRCUIT BOARD TO BOX

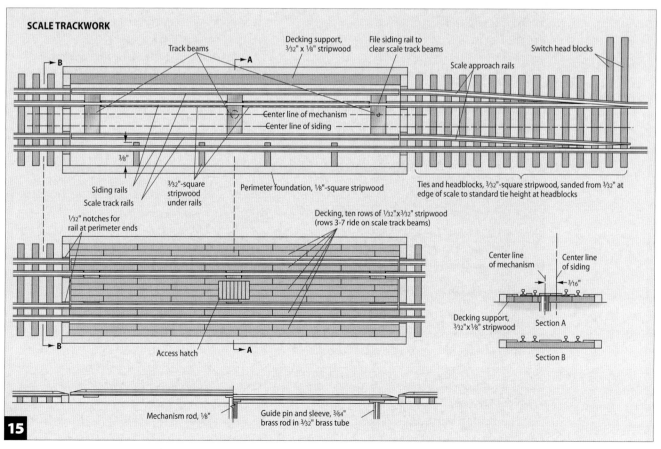

SCALE TRACKWORK

Track beams

Decking support, ³⁄₃₂" x ⅛" stripwood

File siding rail to clear scale track beams

Switch head blocks

B

A

Scale approach rails

Center line of mechanism

Center line of siding

⅜"

Ties and headblocks, ³⁄₃₂"-square stripwood, sanded from ³⁄₃₂ at edge of scale to standard tie height at headblocks

Siding rails

Scale track rails

³⁄₃₂"-square stripwood under rails

Perimeter foundation, ⅛"-square stripwood

¹⁄₃₂" notches for rail at perimeter ends

Decking, ten rows of ¹⁄₃₂"x³⁄₃₂" stripwood (rows 3-7 ride on scale track beams)

Center line of mechanism

Center line of siding

³⁄₁₆"

Decking support, ³⁄₃₂"x⅛" stripwood

Section A

B

Access hatch

A

Section B

Mechanism rod, ⅛"

Guide pin and sleeve, ³⁄₆₄" brass rod in ³⁄₃₂" brass tube

15

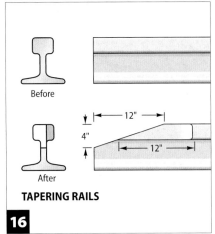

Before

After

12"

4"

12"

TAPERING RAILS

16

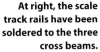

At right, the scale track rails have been soldered to the three cross beams.

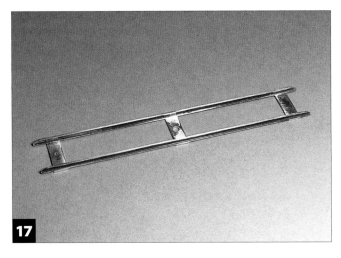

17

Cut the perfboard using the circuit layout as a pattern. Drill ⅛" holes at the three screw locations in the layout (the pads labeled "X"). Back the perfboard with wood while drilling to keep it from chipping.

Tape a copy of the circuit layout to the perfboard. Avoid covering component holes with tape. The component side goes on one side of the perfboard and the trace side on the other. Be sure the top edge (with COM, -M+, and RUN) is aligned on both sides. Make sure the component holes on the diagram align with the holes in the perfboard.

On the trace side, sets of lead holes connected to each other by thick traces are called nets. Each component lead coming through a hole on a net must be connected to every other component on the same net.

As you insert each component, bend its leads to make the necessary connections. Use long-leaded components, like resistors, to connect with short-leaded components, like integrated circuits (ICs), **11**. Be careful to avoid unwanted connections (short circuits) between adjacent nets. When you are finished, soldered leads will cover each circuit trace.

Be aware of polarity-sensitive parts, **12**. The positive terminal of the component is designated with a square lead pad on the circuit diagram.

For the ICs, pins are numbered counterclockwise (viewing from above) starting with pin 1 (see **12**).

Circuit assembly

Add the components to the perfboard. Follow the component-side layout to place each part while inserting its leads through the board. Match component numbers to the parts list (which also lists color coding for the resistors).

For the U1 and U2 op-amp ICs [+], pin 1 is designated with a square pad. If necessary, bend any two opposite-corner pins to hold the ICs in place.

Leave component leads unconnected until all leads for a net are available, then solder all joints on the net at once.

The leads on capacitors C3, C4, and C6 are pre-bent to keep the capacitor standing above the board. Don't pull them down any farther, **13**.

For the LVDT primary and secondary board leads, I simply bent a convenient lead through to the component side of the board and cut it to ½".

I ran out of useful leads on the net connecting pin 6 of U2 with the pin on R16, so I used a short piece of solid 24AWG wire to complete that net.

Part R6, the 22Ω 2W resistor (red-red-black), will get hot during operation, so mount it about ⅜" above the surface of the board.

For transistor Q1, spread the leads slightly to match the holes. This part also gets warm, so mount it about ¼" above the board.

As shown in **13**, I used color-coded 9" lengths of 24AWG solid wire for non-LVDT board connections. Strip these long enough to be used for completing nets on the solder side of the board.

You'll need a power net jumper, a black 24AWG solid wire on the component side of the board connecting the two nets labeled A.

Solder the M+ and M- leads to the proper terminals of the meter.

Circuit testing

Examine the trace side of your circuit board. Look for short circuits between nets, and make sure there are soldered leads corresponding to every net.

Use a volt-ohm-milliammeter (VOM) to check that the power (+5V) lead connects to pin 4 of both U1 and U2. Make sure that the ground (-5V) lead connects to pin 11 on both U1 and U2. If power and ground are reversed to the ICs, they will be destroyed.

18

This empty hopper tips the scale at 18 tons. The switches on the fascia control the points leading to the scale track. The switch at left is set to route the locomotive on the bypass rails.

Adjust R1 to the middle of its range. Apply power from your 5V supply and measure the voltage between pin 1 of U1 and ground. It should be between 2.2 and 2.5 volts.

Clean the ends of the LVDT magnet wire leads by gently squeezing them in 220-grit sandpaper and pulling. Be careful not to break the fine wire. Solder the primary and secondary leads to the PRI and SEC outputs of the circuit board.

Pass the switch leads through the remaining grommeted hole in the box and solder them to switch S1 as shown in **2**. Mount the switch in its hole. Cut six ¼" lengths of vinyl tubing for use as circuit board standoffs, **14**. Close the electrical box with its cover.

Bench tests and adjustments

Set the mode switch (S1) to CAL (calibrate). With R1, R14, and R16 turned to their midpoints, connect the mechanism/circuit assembly to your 5V supply. Wait five minutes for the circuit to warm up, then do the following:

1. Adjust R14 until your meter reads 40 to 60 tons.

2. Adjust R1 for the maximum meter display.

If your meter reads less than 80 tons, you're done. Otherwise return to step 1.

R1 is now set. To adjust R14 and R16, you'll need some test weights and a way to balance them on the ⅛" rod. I waited until the scale track was done, then used it to support a 35mm film canister filled

CIRCUIT BOARD LAYOUT

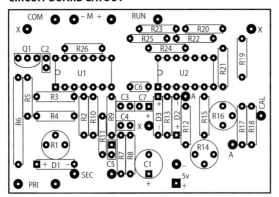

Component side

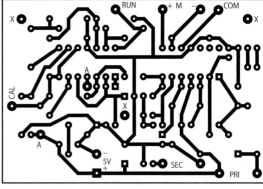

Trace side

Photocopy these circuit layouts and attach them to opposite sides of the perfboard, making sure they are oriented and aligned properly.

with pennies. Pennies weigh .1 ounce, so I used 20 pennies for a two-ounce test and 40 pennies for a four-ounce weight. Adjust R14 and R16 this way:

1. With S1 still set to CAL, turn R14 counter-clockwise until your meter reads 0 tons.

2. Place the two-ounce weight on the mechanism rod.

3. Adjust R16 to 32 tons.

4. Remove the weight.

5. Adjust R14 to zero tons.

6. Replace the two-ounce weight. If your meter reads 32 tons, go to step 7. Otherwise, go back to step 3.

7. Place the four-ounce weight on the mechanism rod.

8. Adjust R16 to 64 tons.

9. Replace the four-ounce weight with the two-ounce weight and check to see that the meter reads 32 tons. If it doesn't, adjust R14 to read 32 tons and go to step 7.

10. Set S1 to RUN. Check that two ounces now reads about 18 tons and four ounces reads about 76 tons. If not, go back to step 2.

Your scale is now adjusted. Unsolder the meter from its leads and you're ready to install your track scale.

Scale track

It's time to build the trackwork, **15**. The parts list is on page 40. You must decide on the length of your scale. Mine is a scale 39 feet, long enough to hold all the wheels of a 40-foot car, but short enough to allow only one car of a string of 34-foot hoppers on the scale at a time.

I used code 83 weathered rail. You can scavenge this from a piece of flextrack. Note that the siding rails are continuous across the scale, unlike the scale and scale approach rails, **15**.

Because of the vertical displacement of the scale, the scale and scale approach rail ends must be tapered, **16**. Cut and carefully file a pair of scale track rails to match. Sand the weathering from the rail bottoms so you can solder them to the brass beams.

Cut three 13⁄16"-long beams from 1⁄32" x 1⁄4" brass bar. Drill a 1⁄8" hole for the mechanism rod in the center beam and a 3⁄64" hole in one end beam for the guide pin. Solder the scale rails to the beams, keeping the rails aligned with track gauges. File the beam ends flush with the rails and file any stray solder from the beams, **17**.

Scale track installation

As shown in section A of **15**, the scale track center is offset 3⁄16" behind the siding track center line. Carefully drill a 7⁄32" hole through your roadbed at this point. This hole must be absolutely vertical. Slide the track scale mechanism/circuit assembly up through this hole. Don't glue it in place—let friction hold the assembly so you can move it around as you install the trackwork.

Solder the scale track to the scale mechanism so the top of the center beam is flush with the top of the mechanism rod. Ensure that the scale assembly is parallel to the track center lines and aligned left to right and front to back.

With the scale track assembly parallel to the track center lines, push the scale track flat against the roadbed and drill a 3⁄64" pilot hole into the roadbed using the guide pin hole as a template. Rotate the scale track out of the way. Drill out the pilot hole to 3⁄32" and install a 1"-long 3⁄32" brass tube flush with the roadbed as the guide pin sleeve. Rotate the scale back into place.

Insert a 1"-long 3⁄64" brass rod guide pin into the hole in the end beam (flush with the top of the beam) and into the 3⁄32" tube. Solder it to the end

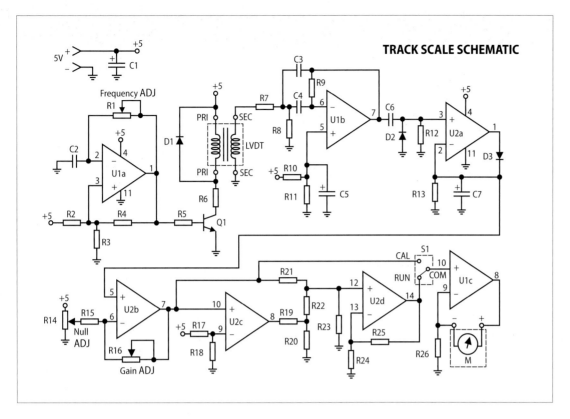

TRACK SCALE SCHEMATIC

beam. Check that the scale track rides up and down on the scale mechanism smoothly and that the guide pin doesn't bind.

Check to see that the deflection of the scale with a loaded hopper (filled with 20 pennies) is about a scale 6".

Install the meter, re-solder the leads, and connect the power supply. Check that an empty hopper displays about 18 tons and a loaded hopper about 76 tons with your scale in "run" mode. If not, repeat the earlier adjustments.

Siding rails

Glue down the ties for the siding and scale approach tracks, **15**. Since the rails ride through the scale ³⁄₃₂" above the roadbed, you'll need to lay ³⁄₃₂"-square ties from the scale's perimeter to the headblock ties at the scale approach switch points (about 25 scale feet). Sand these ties to gradually raise the rail to ³⁄₃₂" at the scale perimeter from the standard ties beyond the head blocks, and stain them.

Frame the scale track with ⅛"-square stripwood. This must be notched to allow both siding and scale approach rails through as in section B. Paint this frame to represent concrete.

Add the front and rear siding rails. These are continuous across the scale. The front rail is spiked to stripwood ties laid every inch or so and out of the way of the moving scale track, **15**. The rear siding rail crosses the three scale track beams, so its bottom plate and part of its web must be filed to clear the beams. The rear rail is glued with CA to ³⁄₃₂"-square stripwood. The ends of the rear rail are filed sharp into switch points for the scale approach switches.

Scale approach rails

The approach rails are simply the last two point rails to complete the scale approach switches. They also must be tapered on the scale track end, **16**. I used Switch Master motors (No. 1001) to operate the switches.

Adjust the empty scale track to ride about a scale 3" above the approach rails by moving the mechanism/circuit assembly beneath the roadbed. You can glue it in place with epoxy from the underside of the roadbed, but mine is held by the friction of the subroadbed.

Detailing

You now have a working track scale, **18**. I added ¹⁄₃₂" x ³⁄₃₂" decking to the scale, **15**. Note that five of the ten courses ride on the scale track as it moves up and down. You may also want to add a thin access hatch in the middle of the scale track.

The final touch is the scale house. Builders In Scale makes a nice model (No. 610). Weather things a bit and your track scale is ready for business!

TRACKWORK

K&S Engineering
126 $\frac{3}{32}$" brass tube
161 $\frac{3}{64}$" brass rod
240 $\frac{1}{32}$" x $\frac{1}{4}$" brass bar

Micro Engineering
16083 code 83 weathered rail (or strip rail from piece of flextrack)

Northeastern Scale Models wood
125 $\frac{1}{32}$" x $\frac{3}{32}$" strip, 3
215 $\frac{3}{32}$"-square strip, 3
216 $\frac{3}{32}$" x $\frac{1}{8}$" strip
231 $\frac{1}{8}$"-square strip

TRACK SCALE MECHANISM

Amidon (240 & 250 Briggs Ave., Costa Mesa, CA 92626, 714-850-4660, www.amidoncorp.com)
R61-025-400 $\frac{1}{4}$" x 4" ferrite rod

K&S Engineering
128 $\frac{5}{32}$" brass tube
129 $\frac{3}{16}$" brass tube
130 $\frac{7}{32}$" brass tube
131 $\frac{1}{4}$" brass tube
132 $\frac{9}{32}$" brass tube
133 $\frac{5}{16}$" brass tube
164 $\frac{1}{8}$" brass rod
240 $\frac{1}{32}$" x $\frac{1}{4}$" brass bar

Radio Shack
64-3025 $\frac{1}{4}$" grommets, 4
278-1345 30-gauge magnet wire

Miscellaneous
2" x 2" x 4" steel electrical switch box
2" x 4" steel switch-box cover
$\frac{5}{16}$" (inside-diameter) nylon washers, 4
ballpoint pen springs, 2
vinyl electrical tape

Circuit Board

Qty.	Symbol	Description (part numbers are Digi-Key* unless noted)
1	R1	10KΩ trim potentiometer (3306P-103-ND)
8	R2, R3, R4, R12, R13, R22, R23, R25	100KΩ resistors [brown-black-yellow] (100KQBK-ND)
1	R5	330Ω resistor [orange-orange-brown] (330QBK-ND)
1	R6	22Ω 2W resistor [red-red-black] (22W-2-ND)
1	R7	3.9KΩ resistor [orange-white-red] (3.9KQBK-ND)
1	R8	1KΩ resistor [brown-black-red] (1KQBK-ND)
1	R9	82KΩ resistor [gray-red-orange] (82KQBK-ND)
4	R10, R11, R15, R19	10KΩ resistors [brown-black-orange] (10KQBK-ND)
1	R14	1KΩ trim potentiometer (3316P-102-ND)
1	R16	1MΩ trim potentiometer (3316P-105-ND)
1	R17	33KΩ resistor [orange-orange-orange] (33KQBK-ND)
1	R18	18KΩ resistor [brown-gray-orange] (18KQBK-ND)
1	R20	8.2KΩ resistor [gray-red-red] (8.2KQBK-ND)
1	R21	180KΩ resistor [brown-gray-yellow] (180KQBK-ND)
1	R24	62KΩ resistor [blue-red-orange] (62KQBK-ND)
1	R26	3.3KΩ resistor [orange-orange-red] (3.3KQBK-ND)
3	D1-D3	diodes (1N4001GICT-ND)
1	C1	1000μF, 10V electrolytic capacitor (P6218-ND)
2	C2, C6	.1μF ceramic capacitors (P4924-ND)
2	C3, C4	.01μF ceramic capacitors (P4922-ND)
1	C5	10μF, 10V electrolytic capacitor (P2026-ND)
1	C7	1μF, 16V electrolytic capacitor (P2105-ND)
1	Q1	2N2222A NPN transistor (PN2222A-ND)
2	U1, U2	LM324 quad op amp ICs (LM324N-ND)
1	M	0-15VDC voltmeter (Radio Shack 270-1754)
1	S1	SPDT toggle switch (Radio Shack 275-613)

Miscellaneous

prepunched perfboard, 2$\frac{3}{4}$" x 6" (Radio Shack 276-1395)
24AWG solid wire
4-40 screws, $\frac{3}{4}$", 3
4-40 nuts, 3
$\frac{1}{8}$" inside diameter, $\frac{3}{16}$" outside diameter vinyl tubing

*Digi-Key, www.digikey.com

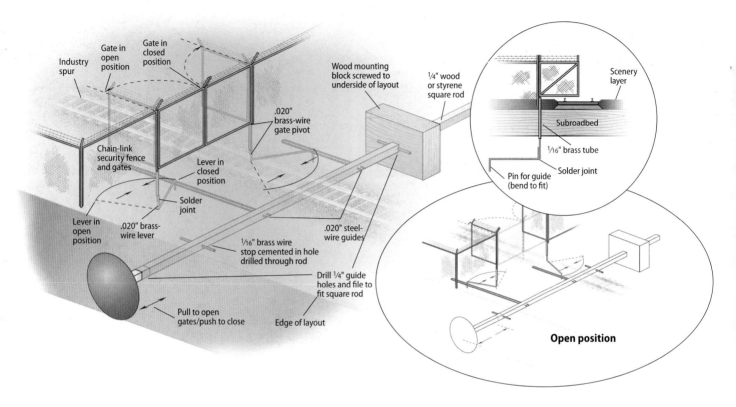

Industry spur

Gate in open position

Gate in closed position

Chain-link security fence and gates

Lever in open position

Lever in closed position

Solder joint

Lever in open position

.020" brass-wire lever

.020" brass-wire gate pivot

¹⁄₁₆" brass wire stop cemented in hole drilled through rod

Pull to open gates/push to close

Edge of layout

.020" steel-wire guides

Drill ¼" guide holes and file to fit square rod

Wood mounting block screwed to underside of layout

¼" wood or styrene square rod

Scenery layer

Subroadbed

¹⁄₁₆" brass tube

Solder joint

Pin for guide (bend to fit)

Open position

Operating gates for industrial spurs

9

By David Popp and Wolfgang Dudler

To protect valuable equipment and commodities, many companies install fences around their property and include swinging gates at key entry points, such as driveways and rail spurs.

A number of manufacturers, including Wm. K. Walthers and Scale Scenics, make good examples of chain link security fences with static gates. Wolfgang Dudler, of Iserlohn, Germany, took the idea a step further. Using a simple square pushrod to move a set of actuating levers, Wolfgang devised the method shown here to operate a set of security gates for one

of his lineside industries. The drawing above shows the basics of the system. When someone needs to set out a car at the plant, he can open the gates by pulling the knob located on the fascia. When the switching work is complete, he can close the gates and secure the factory by pushing the knob back to its starting position.

The gates can easily be incorporated into a layout's operating scheme, with train crews pausing to simulate walking to and unlocking the gate before switching can continue.

The illustration above shows how to make a simple gate mechanism controlled by a push-pull rod.

10 Working 3-position semaphores

By Gary Hoover

Left: The semaphore displays a "clear" aspect for the approaching train. Middle: With the train in the home block, the semaphore displays "stop." Right: The signal remains in the "approach" position until the last car clears the distant block.

The operating semaphore signals on my HO scale Missouri, Kansas & Quincy always attract lots of attention from visitors. Each semaphore, powered by a slow-motion motor, slowly moves to the "occupied" position as a train enters the home block. After the train has completely passed through the home block, the blade slowly rises back to the "clear" position. Real semaphores also have a third ("approach") position, with the blade at a 45-degree angle, to indicate a train two blocks ahead. I designed a simple, reliable device to provide this feature, **1** through **5**.

Semaphores are normally in the vertical ("clear") position if no trains are in the home and distant blocks. The home block is the block of track the semaphore is in and the distant block is the block of track just beyond the home block.

When a train enters the home block, the semaphore blade lowers to the horizontal ("stop") position. When the last car of the train passes out of the home block and into the distant block, the blade rises to approach. When the last car of the train exits the distant block, the blade moves back to clear.

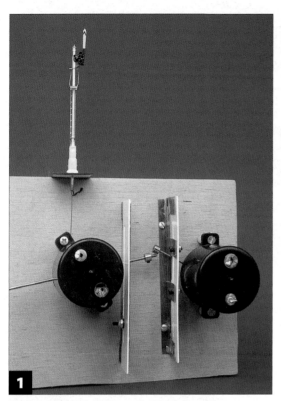

1

This semaphore is in the vertical (clear) position, meaning no trains are present in either the home or distant blocks. The motor for the home block, left, is connected to the semaphore. The distant block motor is at right.

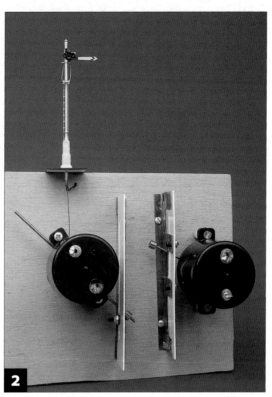

2

When the train enters the home block, the home-block motor lowers the semaphore to the horizontal (occupied or stop) position.

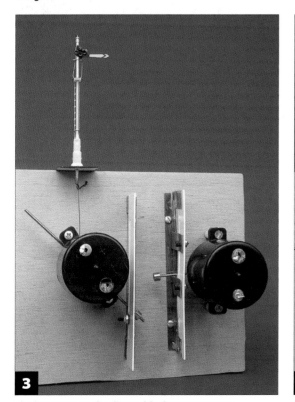

3

The lever arm on the distant block motor rotates counterclockwise as soon as the locomotive enters the distant block. The semaphore blade still shows "occupied," since some of the train is still in the home block.

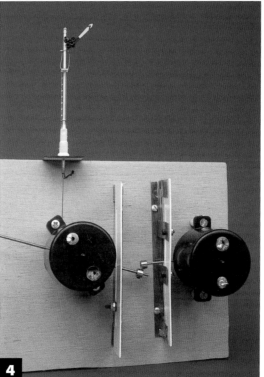

4

When the train clears the home block, the home block motor tries to return to the clear position but is stopped by the distant block's lever arm. This holds the blade at the approach position.

Here's an end view of the mechanism. The home block motor is on the left and the distant block motor is on the right. Aircraft wheel collars hold the lever arms and semaphore blade wire in the correct position.

5

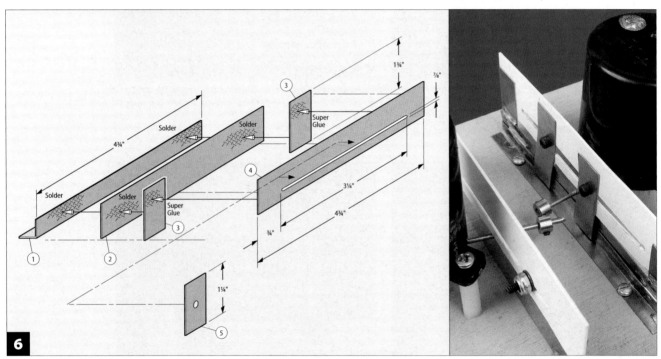

6

Adjustable stops make adjusting the semaphore blade positions quick, easy, and precise.

When a train comes from the opposite direction by entering the distant block first, the semaphore reverts to a two-position signal. The blade moves from clear to occupied as the locomotive passes from the distant block into the home block and remains in the "occupied" position until the entire train has passed through the home block.

The motor connected directly to the semaphore blade responds to the electronic block occupancy detector in the home block. The second motor responds to the detector in the distant block. The arm on the distant block's motor is simply used to block

the arm on the home block's motor from returning to clear when the train passes out of the home block. Switchmaster motors can stall without burning up, so no harm is done by stopping them at any position.

Building the mechanism

Mounting the mechanism on a separate plywood base allows most of the construction work to be done at the workbench rather than under the layout. It's then a simple matter to mount the base to the layout's framework and connect the control rod to the semaphore blade.

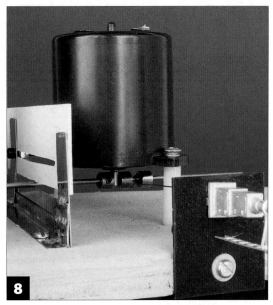

7 The lever arms travel in slots so that they can't ride up and over each other. Aircraft wheel collars on each side of the motor shaft keep the arm in position.

8 A top view of the home block motor shows the semaphore connection to the lever. A small gap between the aircraft wheel collars on each side of the wire allows the wire to pivot when the lever travels through its arc.

The photos and drawings show how everything goes together. Mount the motors (part No. 6) on the base with the center lines of the shafts 3$^{11}/_{16}$" apart. Make sure the lever arms can travel through their required arcs without hitting the mounting standoffs. The mounting standoffs supplied with the motors should be 1$^3/_{16}$" long, **5**, **6**.

Install the lever arms (part No. 7). Aircraft wheel collars (No. 9) keep the arm in position, **7**. I found that the mechanism works best if the distance from the motor shaft to the collar on the end of the lever arm for the home block's motor is slightly longer than that for the distant block's motor. The shorter shaft-to-arm length on the distant block's motor ensures that the home block's lever arm stops solidly when moving from the occupied to the approach position.

The angle assemblies that mount between the two motors are fabricated next, **8**, **9**, **10**. They provide a guide slot in which the lever arm (part No. 7) can travel so that the arms don't ride up and over each other. The angle assemblies also serve as a mounting surface for the adjustable stops (part No. 5).

Making the angle assemblies involves cutting some brass angle (part No. 1), brass strips (Nos. 2, 3, and 5) and styrene strips (No. 4) to the correct sizes. I used a hacksaw and vise to cut the brass angle and tin snips to cut the brass strip. Then I soldered together the angle (part No. 1) and the brass strips (Nos. 2 and 3). The top edge of the completed angle assemblies should just fit under the installed lever arms. I cut the styrene guide strips (No. 4) to size using a hobby

knife. Using styrene for the guide strips rather than brass makes cutting the inside slot easier. I drilled two $^1/_8$" holes to form the ends of the slot and then cut the rest out using a hobby knife and straightedge.

After cutting the guide strips, attach them to the upright strips (part No. 3) using cyanoacrylate adhesive (CA). Position the guide strip just enough above the top of the angle assembly to allow free movement of the $^3/_{32}$"-diameter lever arm. Finally, secure the completed angle assemblies to the wooden mounting base with small screws (part No. 12).

Install the mechanism assembly beneath the layout and connect the semaphore. Bend the end of the thin wire going up to the semaphore blade into a small closed loop. Place the loop over the motor's lever arm on the side opposite the angle assemblies. An aircraft wheel collar placed outside of the wire will keep it in the correct position. Leave a small gap between the collar and the wire so that the wire can pivot slightly rather than bend when the lever arm moves.

Adjust the mechanism by starting with the semaphore blade at vertical. Adjust the distant block's upper stop so that its lever arm just touches the home block's lever arm. Move the home block's lever arm down to where the blade is at horizontal. Move the stop up to where it is just touching the home block's lever arm and tighten the lock bolt. Finally, move the home block's lever arm so the blade indicates approach. Move the distant block's lever arm down until it just contacts the home block's lever arm and set and lock the distant block's lower stop. Once the

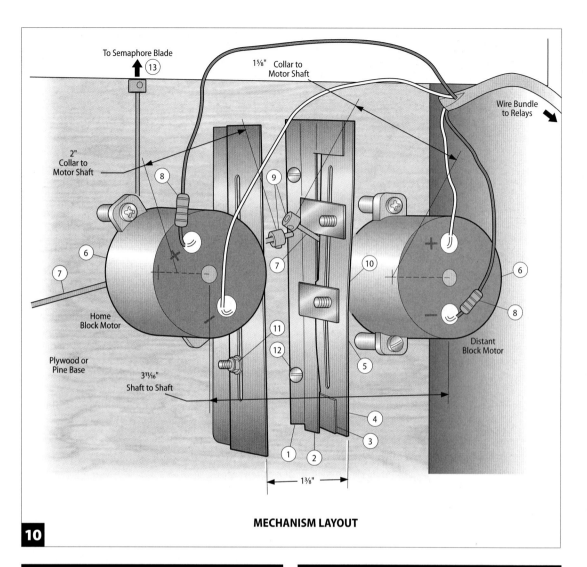

To Semaphore Blade ⑬

1⅝" Collar to Motor Shaft

Wire Bundle to Relays

2" Collar to Motor Shaft

⑧

⑨

⑥

⑦

Home Block Motor

Plywood or Pine Base

3¹¹⁄₁₆" Shaft to Shaft

⑦

⑩

⑥

⑧

Distant Block Motor

⑪

⑫

⑤

④

③

①

②

1⅜"

MECHANISM LAYOUT

10

Bill of Materials

Part No.	Description/ Quantity	Size	Manufacturer/ Item number
1	Brass angle (2)	¼" x ¼" x 4¾"	K&S No. 175
2	Brass strip (2)	1/2" x .025" x 4¾"	K&S No. 236
3	Brass strip— upright (2)	½" x .025" x 1¼"	K&S No. 236
4	Styrene guide strip (2)	4¾" x 1" x .060"	Evergreen No. 9060
5	Brass strip— stop (2)	½" x .025" x 1¼"	K&S No. 236
6	Slow-motion motor (2)	—	Switchmaster
7	Wire-lever arm (2)	³⁄₃₂" x 4"	K&S No. 506 music wire
8	Resistor (2)	1000-ohm, 1-watt	Radio Shack No. 271-153
9	Wheel collars (7)	³⁄₃₂" I.D.	Dubro No. 138

Part No.	Description/ Quantity	Size	Manufacturer/ Item number
9	Wheel collars (7)	³⁄₃₂" I.D.	Dubro No. 138
10	Screw/ washer (3)	4-40 x ¼"	Carl Goldberg No. 502
11	Nut (3)	4-40 self-lock	Dubro No. 170
12	Screw (4)	No. 4 x ½"	Carl Goldberg No. 568
13	Semaphore (1)	—	Tomar No. 853 or No. 854
14	Diode (2)	1 amp, 50 PIV	Radio Shack No. 275-214
15	Wire (1 roll)	22-gauge solid	Radio Shack No. 278-1215
16	Solder (1 roll)	60/40 rosin core	Radio Shack No. 64-005
17	Relay (2)	12-volt DC2	Radio Shack No. 275-214
18	Block detector (2)	—	Circuitron No. BD-1

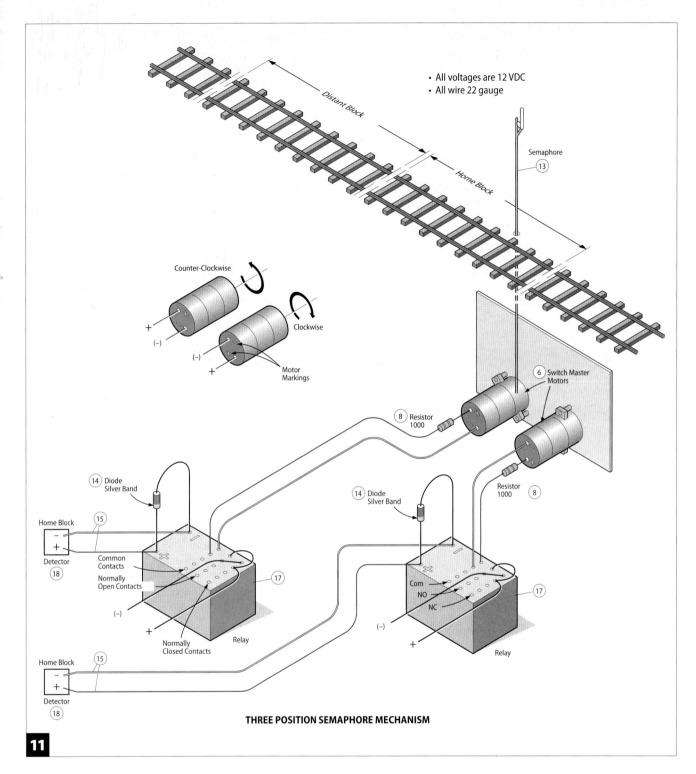

- All voltages are 12 VDC
- All wire 22 gauge

Distant Block

Home Block

Semaphore
(13)

Counter-Clockwise

Clockwise

Motor Markings

(+)
(−)
(−)
(+)

(6) Switch Master Motors

(8) Resistor 1000

Resistor 1000 (8)

(14) Diode Silver Band

(14) Diode Silver Band

Home Block
(15)
−
+
Detector
(18)

Common Contacts

Normally Open Contacts

(−)

+

Normally Closed Contacts

Relay

(17)

Com
NO
NC

(−)

+

Relay

(17)

Home Block
(15)
−
+
Detector
(18)

THREE POSITION SEMAPHORE MECHANISM

11

mechanism is wired and running, a final fine-tuning of the stops might be needed.

Wiring and detection

I use Circuitron's BD1 optical detection system, but any detector that can power a 12-volt DC relay will work. The relay simply switches polarity to the motor; the motor then runs clockwise or counterclockwise. If for some reason the motor runs the wrong way, sim-

ply reverse the wires at the motor. I found the motor speed best with a 1000-ohm, 1-watt resistor.

The diodes on each relay keep electrical spikes in the relay's coil from damaging the block detector.

Solder the wires to the pins on the relay with a small pencil-type iron and thin 60/40 solder.

The realistic indications provided by the semaphore make the short time needed to construct the mechanism well worth it.

11 Add video animation to structures

By D. Derek Verner

There's a party going on in this HO model building, thanks to Derek Verner's video animation techniques.

Most of the time our trains rumble through towns and countryside that are bereft of animation. In fact, when we hear that word we often think of mechanical devices, such as crossing gates, that are herky-jerky and toy-like, but here's a way to add action to a layout with a miniature TV set.

Consider the following: "Can't the trains go any faster?" asks your nonrailroading visitor. Suddenly from the corner of his eye, he catches a flash of movement in one of the illuminated foreground buildings. He steps closer and peers in the window.

Inside, people less than an inch tall are having a party. Couples are dancing and two guys with electric guitars are wailing away. He can hear heavy metal music apparently blaring from their tiny amplifiers.

A light goes on in the apartment next door and a middle-aged couple in bathrobes pound on the adjoining wall. Then the husband strides to his door and steps out. Shortly after, the party's host opens his door in response to insistent knocking. An argument ensues.

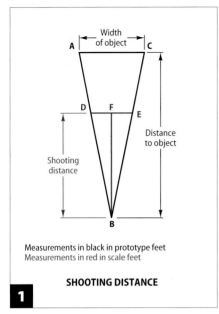

Measurements in black in prototype feet
Measurements in red in scale feet

SHOOTING DISTANCE

1

This will help you calculate shooting distance.

2

The screen can be divided using a grease pencil to allow animation in several different areas.

The visitor turns from the scene in disbelief. "Are those kids having another party?" you casually inquire. The party-goers are video images you've reproduced on a miniature TV set concealed within the structure. A VCR feeds the signal from a tape starring your friends and family.

What you'll need

You can use a VCR to feed signals to the TV. The next item is a video camera or camcorder. You only need the camera during production and can borrow or rent it. The last major item is a mini-TV. These are available in black and white or color, with screen diagonals of 1.6" to 5". You can install the set so it can be easily removed to watch the ball game.

Most of the mini color sets are LCD (liquid crystal display) types and are highly directional. If you look at them off-axis, strange things happen to brightness and contrast. For this reason, special precautions must be taken to control the angle of viewing which are described later in the mini-TV installation section.

A better image is produced by a CRT (cathode ray tube) display like those used on standard TV sets. Unfortunately, I haven't been able to find a CRT color set with a screen smaller than 5". Surprisingly though, black and white is very effective.

Getting started

Step 1 is hooking up the camera to the mini-TV. Follow the instructions that come with the camera.

Once you're getting the image on the TV from the camera, prepare a diagram like the one in **1**. If your video camera is equipped with a zoom lens, set it to its widest angle. Point the camera at a distant object that fills the screen from side to side, then measure the distance from the object to the camera lens.

Next, measure the width of the object. Use these two measurements to construct triangle A-B-C in the scale you model. This represents the widest angle of view to which your camera can be set. Next measure the width of your screen in your modeling scale and transfer this measurement to the diagram, shown as line D-E. Now, measure line B-F in scale feet. This distance (in real feet) is how far your camera must be from the subject to produce an image on the screen that is in proper scale.

For most cameras this distance is longer than most rooms, an obvious difficulty when it comes to producing your tape. There are solutions:

You can add an auxiliary wide-angle adapter lens available from video suppliers, or you can shoot in a theater, gymnasium, or outdoors using the side of a building as a backdrop.

The final suggestion, which will be discussed next, is to use the camcorder to tape partial frame images from a regular TV playing the original tape. Because

Video update

Video technology has advanced significantly since this item first appeared in December 1996, but the ideas and concepts are still very much valid, and the range of products now available makes it much easier to accomplish these things. You can find old VCRs and CRT televisions at bargain prices, or you can apply these techniques using computer video editing and computer screens.

A matte box fitted to the front of the camera (mounted in front of the lens at left) permits shooting images confined to particular areas on the tape.

3

Derek built an .080" styrene box to fit snugly over and hold this mini-TV set. The box was then mounted inside an HO scale building.

4

A "room" added to the front of the box controls the angle at which the screen can be viewed.

5

our final image is so small, the decrease in quality will not be noticeable.

Multiple images

To create the party scene described earlier you'll want activity in two rooms, so you'll need to divide the screen into different areas. I did this for four areas, **2**.

I started by attaching a matte box attached to the front of a video camera, **3**. With such a box you can block out portions of the image during taping. On mine a sliding panel and a piece of black cardboard

can be adjusted to mask out the portions of the screen that are to remain dark. You can jury-rig something out of cardboard. Be sure the inside is black and the mattes are far enough away from the lens to produce a sharp edge when the camera is focused on the subject.

Since our goal is to produce four areas where animated images can appear, we don't need to tape our original footage from such a great distance after all, as we'll be reshooting off the TV screen. Since each scene represents a fourth of the mini-TV's screen area, it can be shot from half the distance.

If you choose this method, the original tapes should be shot without the matte box so they fill the viewfinder. When you reshoot them from the large TV screen onto the four different areas, you can do it in a darkened room, and again the matte box won't be needed.

Mini-TV installation

Now decide what sort of model building will house the TV set. Will it be an office, factory, or apartment? It must be large enough to house the mini-TV with the screen set back from the windows.

Design a method to hold the TV in position yet allow it to be removed easily. The box and room shown in **4** and **5** are examples of ways to help control the angle of viewing. You can provide access from beneath the layout or design the building so it can be lifted off its foundation. Provide paths for the power cable (usually a wall transformer) and the signal cable. If your VCR needs to be in another room, you can run cable or use a wireless transmitter.

The television image in **6** is from a black-and-white CRT, and while I was pleased with the clarity of the images, I didn't care for the "color"—it appeared too blue. For this reason, and to provide variety in the lighting of the four areas, I used different theatrical gels (which are available at theatrical and photography supply stores) on the windows of each apartment. Browns and ambers worked well and warmed up the scenes to make the lighting appear incandescent.

Shooting the production

The animation scenario you decide to shoot should be short—no longer than a minute or two—and it should contain as much action and movement as possible. Show the kids playing with the dog, someone vacuum cleaning, or a forklift being driven around a warehouse. It's the movement that will attract the visitor to the window.

Set the camera on a tripod or other stable support at about eye level. Tape speed should be standard, or SP, because our final tape will be second generation and we want to preserve as much image quality as possible.

If your camera is far from the action, you can place a microphone in the scene to pick up the sounds.

The idea is to shoot one or more short sequences and then loop them to create a final two-hour tape with random intervals of action. It's the lights going on and off and flashes of movement that catch your eye. You can have one of your actors flip a wall switch at the beginning and end of each sequence to justify the effect.

Keep props and sets as simple as possible. This is particularly true if you include three-dimensional objects in the room, 5. If it doesn't move or get moved, leave it out. This also simplifies shooting if you are forced outdoors to use the side of a building as a backdrop.

Making the final tape

Since the final production tape will run for two hours with the action taking place at intervals, it's essential that the screen go dark between these intervals. Blank tape played on a VCR produces a raster pattern. Therefore, the final tape must be prerecorded with "video black." To prepare your final tape, leave the audio cables disconnected, rewind the tape, place the lens cap on the camera, press RECORD on the VCR and let it run to the end.

Reconnect the audio cables, rewind the tape, and locate the first sequence you want to copy onto the final tape. Press PLAY on the camcorder and RECORD on the VCR to copy the sequence. When it's over, stop the VCR and camcorder and find the second sequence or rewind the camcorder to the beginning of the same sequence. Press PLAY or FAST FORWARD on the VCR for an interval of black. Repeat until the tape is filled.

All that remains is to connect the VCR to your TV and play your masterwork. If you use sound, keep the volume at a low level. It should only be audible once your visitor's attention has been drawn to the scene.

The technical side of making videos can be confusing at first, but the process is quite fascinating. The late, great Orson Welles was once asked how he liked making films. Reaching for the ultimate complimentary metaphor, he replied, "It's the greatest train set a boy can have."

6

A wood block holds the TV set in its frame (left). Since even small LCD television sets generate some heat, it's best to leave the glazing out of most windows to allow the heat to escape. Theatrical or photo gel samples can be used to change the apparent color of the illumination in the room. A black-and-white TV image without gels (right) has a blue tinge.

Lou Sassi

12 Loading and unloading coal

By Jeff Ashby, Don Ball, and Jeff Needham

An operator working at Ashco Mine in Erika Falls stops to load empty hoppers. Jeff Ashby designed a mechanical system that he uses for the coal loaders at three mines on his N scale Logan Subdivision.

The Ashco Mine at Erika Falls is one of three scratchbuilt mines on Jeff Ashby's N scale layout that feature an operating coal loader, **1**, **2**. The illustration, **3**, and photos show the Ashco Mine, but all the mines use the same type of loading system.

The overhead building houses a storage bin for the coal. This building's roof is removable. The loading system is hidden under the layout and behind the rock face next to the mine. A wood tab attached to a hinge is mounted on the fascia. Fishing line runs from the tab through the eyelet of a lead fish-

ing weight and is attached to an eye screw under the layout. The fishing weight is also attached to .020" steel rod. The other end of the rod is twisted around brass bar stock. Mounted on a pivot, the bar stock is wide enough to cover an opening in the bottom of the coal storage bin.

An operator positions an empty hopper under the loader's apron and then pulls the fascia-mounted tab. This action tightens the fishing line, which pushes the steel rod up. The steel rod forces the bar to swing down on its pivot, opening the spout of

2

Coal runs from the loader into the hopper car. Keep the opening small enough to enable the operator to easily control the amount delivered to each car.

the coal storage bin. The coal then pours out of the apron opening.

Once the hopper is full, the operator pushes the tab toward the fascia, making the fishing line go slack. The lead weight then pulls the steel rod down, causing the bar to close the spout.

Rotary coal dumper

The hopper car unloading shed at Nverno Power is removable, **4**. Inside that structure is an operating rotary coal dumper that I scratchbuilt, **5**.

The track inside the shed is attached to a movable piece of plywood mounted on a pivot. I cut an opening in the subroadbed and placed a bin underneath the layout to catch the loose coal.

The parts called the lock bar and lock bar tower in the illustration hold the hopper in place. These are made from wood. The lock bar is attached to the lock bar tower with a dowel, which also allows the lock bar to pivot. Fishing line attached to the end of the lock bar runs under the pivoting roadbed and continues under the layout to a spool attached to a wood platform on the fascia.

Once an operator spots and uncouples a single loaded hopper inside the unloading shed, he turns the crank on the spool counterclockwise. The fishing line pulls the lock bar tight against the top of the

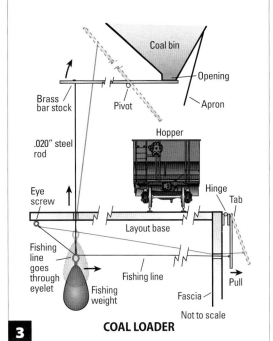

3 **COAL LOADER**

Not to scale

Jeff Ashby built his coal loader in N scale, but his design could easily be applied to loaders in other scales as well.

hopper. A piece of foam rubber keeps the wood lockbar from damaging the car. As the operator continues turning the crank, the roadbed and hopper pivot, emptying the coal into the bin.

With the car now empty, the operator turns the crank in the opposite direction. A counterweight

The rotary dumper is inside the shed, which is easily lifted off the layout for maintenance. A bin under the layout catches the coal when it's dumped.

4

Both photos: Lou Sassi

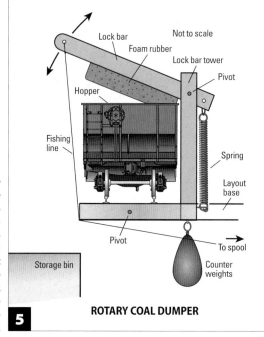

The fishing line that controls the mechanism wraps around a spool with a crank on the layout's fascia. The spring and counterweight bring the track on the pivoting section back to alignment with the track entering the rotary dumper.

Labels in diagram: Lock bar · Not to scale · Foam rubber · Lock bar tower · Pivot · Hopper · Fishing line · Spring · Layout base · Pivot · To spool · Counter weights · Storage bin

5

ROTARY COAL DUMPER

helps bring the pivoting roadbed into the upright position. A spring helps lift the lock bar off the top of the hopper. A locomotive then removes the hopper from the shed.

Several sizes of scale coal are available from Highball Products, Scenic Express, and Woodland Scenics, but Jeff chose to use real coal on his layout. He crushes the coal in a coffee can with a heavy steel rod, then sifts the coal through a tea strainer. The finished result is a uniform size that easily passes through the mines' loading chutes.

A working flood loader

When Jeff Needham built a flood loader for his HO layout, **6**, he wanted something simple and robust enough to withstand the layout section that it rests upon being repeatedly set up, taken down, and stored. The sides of the structure are foam core, sheathed in Evergreen styrene siding. The roof is more foam core with styrene, and is removable so that the loader can be filled with scale coal. Two more pieces of foam core glued inside the structure form the sloped bottom of the bin itself. The two halves of the bottom are spaced about ¼" apart to form the gate opening.

Jeff kept the bin's mechanism simple as well. A piece of styrene slides across the bottom of the bin to act as the gate. It slides in a groove formed by two styrene strips at either edge. A small dowel extending through the front wall of the loader acts as an operating handle. A short piece of rubber tubing slips over this dowel to provide a better grip for the operator. With the tube removed, the dowel is fairly inconspicuous and doesn't detract from the loader's appearance.

Operations follow the same process as a real flood loader. To operate the model loader, a crewman pulls the gate open as the train continuously (and slowly) moves under the bin, and then shuts it at the right time between cars. The first time this was tried, piles of spilled coal stopped the loading after about three cars. Two things were wrong: there wasn't enough light under the bin to really see where the gondola was, and the spilled coal needed someplace to go.

Both problems were easily solved. To get enough light, Jeff used structural styrene girders to build a small truss below the bin. To this, he attached three micro light bulbs. Besides enabling the operator to see the tops of the gondolas and the flowing coal, the lights also make the structure more attractive.

6

Pulling on a piece of rubber tube opens the flood loader, allowing the coal to fall into the railcar. When not in use the tube is removed, leaving just an unobtrusive nub that doesn't detract from the loader's appearance.

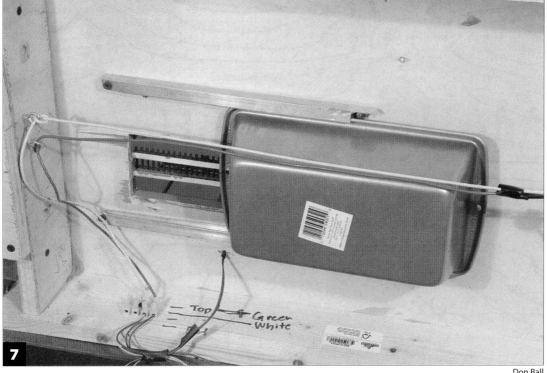

7

To keep spilled coal from piling up on the tracks, Jeff Needham cut away the roadbed beneath the loader and installed a bread pan that slides in place on a pair of metal rails. Any stray coal that misses a gondola simply falls into the pan.

The second problem was solved by attaching a bread pan below the layout, **7**. Jeff cut a hole in the roadbed and subroadbed directly below the loader. He laid two stringers across this hole to support the track, and then attached two lengths of ⅜" aluminum channel below the grade. The bread pan easily slides into place on these channels. Now, any excess coal simply falls into the pan, which can be slid out and its contents emptied back into the loading bin. The hole in the roadbed turns out to be almost invisible, since it's effectively hidden by the structure and the cars.

Jeff discovered a side benefit to modeling a working flood loader with real coal. Coal dust weathering is automatically applied to the structure and surrounding area, just like the prototype.

13 Modeling platform and building lights

By Cody Grivno

Adding lights to an existing scene is a project that can be completed in a couple of evenings. Cody Grivno illuminated the town of Mukwonago on the HO Milwaukee, Racine & Troy.

Real railroads operate around the clock, meaning that we can add night operations to our model railroads. One of the ways we can make our "nighttime" operating sessions more realistic is by adding lights to structures, vehicles, and station platforms. Here's how I illuminated Mukwonago on the Kalmbach employee club layout, the HO scale Milwaukee, Racine & Troy.

Adding lights to an existing scene requires planning up front, so draw a diagram to see how your proposed lighting project will work.

When working on a wiring project, be prepared for surprises. For example, the lights over the Mukwonago station signs shown in step 4 operate at a lower voltage than the rest of the lights and require resistors. After installation, I tested them, and the filaments on these bulbs were barely glowing. After talking with editor Neil Besougloff and executive editor Andy Sperandeo, we determined the supplied resistors for those bulbs weren't right for our application.

Fortunately, Andy knew we had a decade box (available from Mouser) for testing resistors. It turns

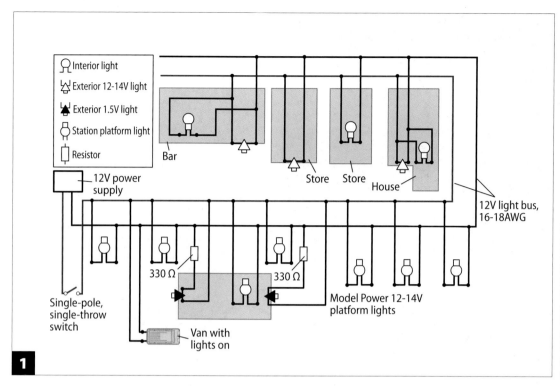

1

Determine the number and types of lights you need for your scene. Drawing a plan helps determine the amount of power you'll need. This area is controlled by a single on/off switch, but you can add additional switches if desired.

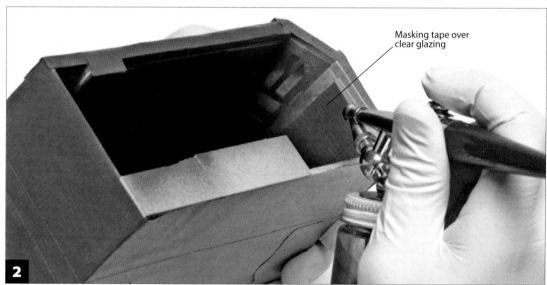

2

Masking tape over clear glazing

Airbrushing interior walls black will eliminate light showing through the plastic. Be sure to mask off windows and doors.

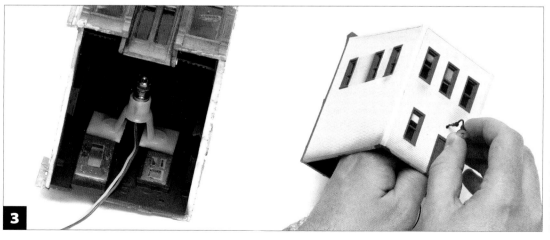

3

Mount interior lights high enough so they can't be seen through windows. Building-mounted exterior lights help illuminate the scene as well as the structure.

The Busch minivan with working headlights adds a great deal to the scene. Cody also added Miniatronics lamps above the station signs on the depot. The wires from the interior and exterior lights of the house at far right are soldered together.

4

out the supplied 470-ohm resistor was too strong for our circuit. We needed a ⅛-watt, 330-ohm resistor instead.

Lighting projects require patience and attention to detail, so work carefully. In the end, you'll be rewarded with a scene that will be a real attention getter.

Drafting a plan

As with any project, it's good to have a plan of attack before starting. David Popp developed the wiring outline and diagram shown in **1** for our Mukwonago scene.

You'll notice that on the house and bar, which have two lights each, there is only one set of wires that connect to the bus. That's because I wired the bulbs together inside the structures, giving me fewer feeder wires to deal with under the layout. I wired these lights in parallel.

We'll get into more detail on wiring the structures, but first let's get the structures ready.

Preparing the buildings

I didn't want to illuminate each and every structure window, which would be unrealistic. To prevent light from shining through windows, I masked off select windows with Scotch-Blue painter's tape, **2**, and then sprayed the interior of each building with Polly Scale Steam Power Black. The dark paint not only prevents light from shining through the windows, it keeps light from glowing through the plastic walls too.

Installing the lights

Next, I added lights to the buildings. I used Brawa No. 3415 bulbs for the interior lights, **3**. To keep the bulbs (and bases) out of sight, I mounted them above the doors and windows with double-sided foam tape. I ran the wires between the doors and windows so they wouldn't dangle in front of the clear glazing.

I used Walthers and Miniatronics lamps for the exterior lights. Before I installed the Walthers lamps

(No. 933-1094), I measured 5/16" above the selected doors. At that height, I marked the center of the door, then drilled a 1/8" opening for the wires. I cemented the lamp to the building with cyanoacrylate adhesive (CA).

Vehicle and station lights

Since the scene includes a commuter station, there are plenty of vehicles in the lot. I thought it would be neat to have at least one vehicle with its headlights and taillights on, **4**. Busch produces a Chrysler minivan that has such features. Like the building lights, the van has two wires that I attached to the lighting bus.

I installed the Miniatronics lamps (No. 72-315-03) above the station signs on the depot using the same technique (but a smaller drill bit) shown earlier. These 1.5V lights needed resistors to be used with our 12V) power supply. I used a 1/8 W, 330-ohm resistor with each lamp as shown in the diagram in step 1.

The house has an interior and exterior light. To reduce the number of feeder wires I'd need to attach to the bus, I soldered the wires from the Brawa light to those from the Walthers lamp. Both the insulation and the wire on the lamp leads are delicate, so use care when stripping the ends for soldering.

Power source

The lights are powered by a 12V, 1.5-amp power supply (RadioShack No. 273-1775). I first removed the adapter plug with a pair of wire cutters, **5**. Then I pulled the two wires apart. The strand with the numbers is the negative and is attached to the bus. The strand with the dashed lines is positive and is attached to a single-pole single-throw (SPST) switch.

Dropping the wires

The scenery base at Mukwonago is a mixture of plywood and extruded-foam insulation board. I marked the locations where the wires would pass through the layout and drilled holes at these spots. To make it easier to feed the wires through the foam and plywood, I inserted small coffee straws, **6**, into the holes and fed the wires through the smooth straws.

Wiring connections

To reduce the amount of soldering I'd have to do beneath the layout, I used 3M ScotchLok insulation displacement (suitcase) connectors, **7**, which are available from Mouser, Micro-Mark, and most hardware and home improvement stores. The connectors

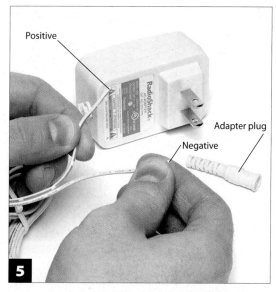

5

A "wall-wart" type plug-in power supply provides electricity to light the scene.

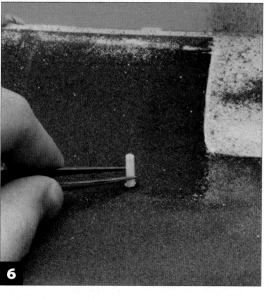

6

Adding a small straw makes it easier to pass wires through a hole drilled in the layout surface.

are offered for various gauges of wire, so select the ones that are appropriate for your project.

To use the connectors, I placed the 18AWG bus wire into the top connector. Then I slid the feeder into the bottom opening. Once the wires were in place, I used a ScotchLok Crimping Tool (a pair of pliers would also work) to press the metal connecting bar into place. Once that was set, I snapped the plastic cover over the connector.

The wires from the lights are too thin to work with the ScotchLok connectors. I rectified this situation by using 18AWG stranded copper wire to transition from the suitcase connectors to the wires from the lights.

I made a loop at the end of the 18AWG wire and tinned it. Then I ran the stripped end of the thin wire through the opening and wrapped it around the heavier-gauge wire. It's important to form a

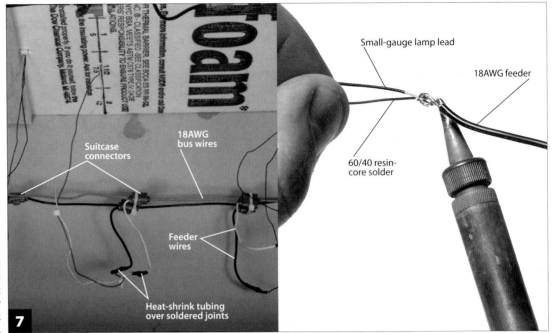

Insulation displacement connectors (IDCs), also called suitcase connectors, are used to connect lamps to the power bus. The lamp wires must first be soldered to heavier (18AWG) wire to work with the IDCs.

7

Suitcase connectors

18AWG bus wires

Feeder wires

Heat-shrink tubing over soldered joints

Small-gauge lamp lead

18AWG feeder

60/40 resin-core solder

Check structures for light leaks at their bases. Wetting the foam and then pressing the house (right) firmly into place took care of a leak around its foundation. A small piece of foam glued inside the base took care of a leak under the rear door of the structure at far right.

8

Foam

good mechanical joint before applying the solder. To prevent a cold joint (one not heated long enough to activate the bond between the wires and molten solder), I applied the heat on the larger side of the wire splice, and then touched the solder to the opposite side until it melted and flowed in.

Putting it to the test

With all of the wiring complete, it was time to make a final inspection with the overhead lights turned off, **8**. All of the model lights worked, but I discovered two light leaks. The leak at the base of

the house was easy to fix. I soaked the ground foam with isopropyl alcohol to reactivate the scenery adhesive and pressed the house back into the foam, as shown above.

However, the leak at the base of the store shown above couldn't be fixed the same way. The garbage cans helped conceal some of the light. To prevent the light from glowing under the door, I had to improvise. I used full-strength white glue to attach a small dark gray foam block by the door. Much like weatherstripping stops drafts, the foam stops light leaks.

Photos by Lloyd Loring

Add lights to your structures

14

By John Underhill

Interior lighting adds another level of realism to the buildings on a layout. The effect of interior lighting is magical in a darkened train room when the only visible light comes from the windows and doorways of town buildings and rural structures. The effect becomes even more exciting as the headlight of a speeding locomotive flashes past in the darkness.

To capture this realism, it's important to think about a prototype building's appearance at night—a large office building might have lights on only in the lobby and one occupied office. A house might have a light on in only one bedroom. On the other hand, a large industrial plant that operates 24 hours a day will be fully illuminated. However, if the plant has only a day shift, its lights will be off at night except for the loading dock.

Once you've figured out what activities need to continue through the night, you can determine the number of light bulbs you'll need to install.

Intensity makes a difference

Close observation of buildings at night reveals that

As twilight fades into darkness, the realism of John Underhill's HO layout is enhanced by the structure lighting that illuminates store display windows, apartment interiors, and other centers of activity.

the rooms display different levels of light, **1**. You can easily alter the brightness of lamps by operating 12-, 14-, or 16-volt bulbs with a 12-volt power supply. The different lamp ratings mean they'll deliver varying intensities of light.

You can also control the intensity of the light by placing bulbs at varying distances from the windows, using different sizes of bulbs, and making rooms of varying sizes. Adding white styrene or painting the walls white behind the bulb, **2**, or installing a white ceiling reflects more light and raises the intensity of light in a room.

The best time to install interior lighting is while the building is under construction. I install the bulbs after I've completed the structure's floor and exterior walls, but before adding the roof. At this point access to the interior is easy. Lighting can also be installed in a finished building by removing its roof or floor.

Concealing the source

The view into a building is important, because you don't want visitors to see a bright bulb inside. To avoid this problem, I place each building on the layout and mark its exact location so I can return it to the same place.

Look for interior locations where a bulb can be concealed from view. Then check the location by looking into the windows and open doors from every possible viewing angle. I also look at the building from different heights, by bending down or using a stool.

Once satisfied, I mark the hidden bulb locations on the floor of the building. Then I check under the layout to be sure nothing will be damaged when I drill the holes for the wiring.

One room at a time

For modeling purposes, I call each interior space that will be illuminated a room. This room can be the entire building or just a portion of it.

I carefully check each room for light leaks at the corners, ceiling and floor joints, and around the window and door frames. Many of my model buildings didn't include floors, so I made my own from wood or styrene sheet.

To check for light leaks, I use a flashlight or a 12-volt bulb with 18" wire leads connected to a power pack. The long lead wires let me slip the lamp inside the structure so I can easily check all the joints.

This is also a good time to check the walls. Some building walls are so thin that light shows through. If this happens, I either paint the interior walls flat black or add another layer of material to make them thicker.

If a building has several rooms, I give the same attention to all the walls and joints to avoid any light leaks.

Beware of light on the sky

Sometimes the light from a window will fall on the backdrop. Raising or relocating the bulb will often solve the problem. I've also had to close a few windows by covering their openings from the inside with wood or styrene painted flat black on both sides.

Windows that face away from the viewer can be used to produce a handy footlight effect. I cut an opening in the back of the building and install a bulb inside that will illuminate the area behind the building. If necessary, I add a false wall to mask the bulb from the balance of the interior. (Evergreen

The need for interior details depends upon the viewing distance. At moderate distances (4 to 6 feet), interior details won't be seen, so lightly frosted plastic windows will block the view into an empty room. Painting the walls flat black and adding a hidden bulb will provide some variety.

At closer viewing distances, a few simple details will provide the illusion of activity inside a room. One trick I use is to place a pair of figures just inside a window, facing each other, as though they're having a conversation.

Adding visible details inside rooms can be fun and doesn't have to take a lot of time. In HO and N scales, there's no need to superdetail desks with miniature pencils and paper clips. All you need to do is create an impression, and the viewer's imagination will fill in the details. I simulate furniture with small wood blocks painted in light colors to contrast with the walls. I place this "furniture" near the windows and then add a figure or two in front to distract the viewer's eye.

Adding color to the walls of the rooms attracts attention because light reflects off the walls. If the viewer is close enough to look inside, light-colored walls work well, but then the room will need to be detailed.

An angled view shows only a small portion of the interior wall. In these cases, I glue a framed picture on the light-colored wall and finish off the room with a figure looking out the window.

A vertical tube supports most lightbulbs inside John's buildings. The white walls behind the lamp reflect light in one direction, while an extra layer of styrene keeps light from showing through the thin plastic walls.

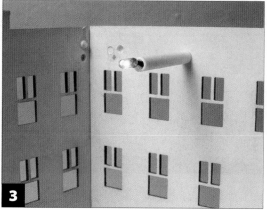

On tall buildings, bulbs can be supported by horizontal tubes through the side or back walls. After the light tube is in place, John adds floors and other interior partitions to direct the light into specific rooms.

sells black styrene sheet that's perfect for this job.) In this case, I'm careful to ensure that the additional exterior light doesn't show on the backdrop.

Replaceable bulbs

It's desirable to be able to replace a bulb without having to take a building from the layout or lift off its roof. To keep the bulbs accessible, I mount them on vertical lengths of Plastruct No. 228 ³⁄₁₆" styrene tubing, **2**. Each removable tube passes through the layout and the building's floors to support a bulb at the correct height.

Using my bulb location mark, I drill a ³⁄₁₆"-diameter hole through the floor of the building. Then I reposition the building on the layout and use the ³⁄₁₆"-diameter hole in the floor to locate a ¼"-diameter hole through the layout.

To determine the length of the tubing, I measure the lamp's elevation inside the building, add the layout's thickness, and add about ¼" to provide room to tape the lamp's wires to the tube.

After measuring the tube's length, I record it beneath the building on the underside of the layout. I also include the name of the building and the length of the tube near the spot where the tube comes through the layout. Remember, the bulb must

pass completely through the tube and protrude ½" beyond its end to ensure full illumination and avoid overheating. Then I cement the tube into the floor of the building.

To light the upper floors of my taller buildings, I use horizontal instead of vertical tubes. They enter the tall buildings from the back where they're out of sight, **3**.

As before, the bulb should protrude about ½" beyond the end of the tube. The wires from the bulb are run down the rear wall of the building.

With all of my bulb leads exiting under the layout, I connect all the wires to Radio Shack No. 274680 terminal strips with screw terminals.

Most of my bulbs are Micro-Mark No. 82590 C grain-of-wheat bulbs, 12- or 14-volt ⅛"-diameter bulbs, or Miniatronics No. 1801420 2.4mm, 14-volt lamps. The wires on these bulbs are long enough and stiff enough for the bulbs to be easily pushed up through the tubing and to be held in position.

Other manufacturers offer lamps in a variety of colors, sizes, and voltages that can be used for all sorts of special effects. In addition, light-emitting diodes offer even more options. All it takes is a bit of imagination and some ingenuity to add your own realistic lighting effects.

Photos by the author

15 Lighting scenes on your model railroad

By Paul J. Dolkos

This Rayon plant, built by Richard Daniels and shown on Jim Brewer's HO Norfolk & Western layout, has nearly 500 miniature light bulbs.

We appreciate the glow of a locomotive's headlight and trackside signals, so why not extend that appeal throughout our layouts? Scenic lighting can range from a fully illuminated industrial complex, such as the one shown above, to a single lighted window in a house. Scenic lighting isn't difficult to install. It's just a matter of connecting multiple low-voltage bulbs.

No matter what type of scenic lighting you want to use, you need to plan for it before you start building structures or adding scenery to your layout.

Types of bulbs

There are a variety of miniature bulbs that can be used for scenic lighting. They're typically rated from 1.5 to 14 volts (V). The tiny 1.5V bulbs are delicate and should be reserved for special applications where size is critical, such as a marker light on a chimney or tall antenna mast, **1**. Otherwise, use a standard bulb voltage so you're always certain what power is required.

Richard Daniels, who lighted and built the rayon plant shown above, recommends 12V bulbs. These long-lasting bulbs provide a lot of light and are offered in various colors and sizes.

One common bulb size is "grain-of-wheat," ⅛" (about 3mm) in diameter. Another common small size is "grain-of-rice," 3⁄32" (about 2mm) in diameter. There are also 5mm-diameter lamps, **2**.

In addition to incandescent bulbs, which lend a pleasing warm color to a model scene, there are miniature fluorescent lamps, fiber-optic strands, and bright light-emitting diodes (LEDs).

Power supplies

One or more power supplies will be required for scenic lights on a layout. Though any power supply with an output that matches the bulb voltage will work, Richard recommends using a regulated supply because it suppresses power line surges. This significantly increases the life of the bulbs.

Power supplies must also be able to handle the current required for the number of bulbs used. Miniature bulbs typically draw from 30 to 80 milliamps (mA). The basic math is that with one amp (1000mA) of current, with loading conservatively at 80 percent of capacity as a safeguard, ten 80mA lamps can be powered. So for an urban scene with numerous lights, a 3-amp or larger supply is recommended. Separate power supplies are ideal if you have several illuminated scenes.

Power supplies are available from electronic suppliers listed on page 69, including All Electronics, Mouser, Parts Express, and RadioShack, as well as some of the model lighting manufacturers. If you operate sound-equipped locomotives, be aware that some of the high-current power supplies have cooling fans that emit noise that may compete with your locomotives.

Model railroad power packs can also be used as a direct-current (DC) power source, but many aren't regulated. Since the voltage level varies when using the speed control, it's possible to accidently increase the voltage beyond the bulb rating. Small alternating current (AC) power adapters usually have limited current output. Though many of these aren't regulated either, they can be used to power a handful of bulbs.

In one instance I connected the bulbs in a station to my Digital Command Control (DCC) power bus because it was readily available and the building was the only lighted structure on the layout. However, having several bulbs connected to the power bus isn't recommended, as they could impose a significant current draw on the system and make it difficult to operate trains.

1

Three red 1.5V bulbs add to the realism of the communication tower on Bill Day's layout. Such bulbs are delicate and should be used only where their small size is necessary.

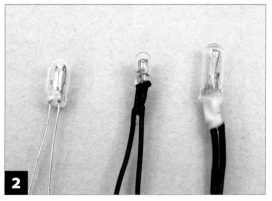

2

All Electronics' grain-of-wheat bulb (14V, 40mA) and Micro-Mark's grain-of-rice (12V, 30mA) and 5mm grain-of-wheat (12V, 82mA) bulbs can all be used for scenic lighting. These bulbs range in price from 40 cents to $1 each.

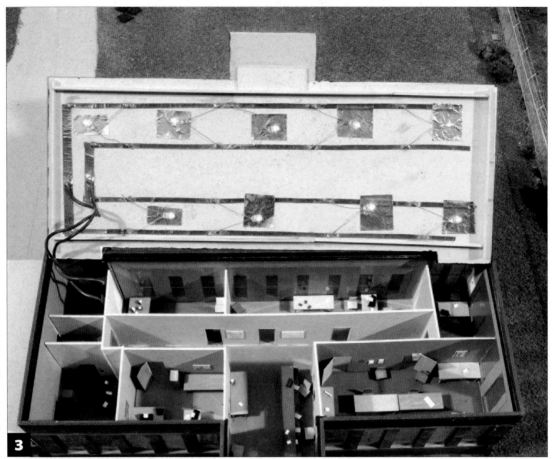

To suggest the lights are on in some rooms but not others, Richard Daniels built wall partitions from thick styrene sheet. He painted the walls to prevent the light from glowing through the styrene.

3

Since the freight dock and office are illuminated, Bill Day added some basic details to these two rooms. The John Deere simulated neon window sign on the right is from Miniatronics.

4

Since you probably won't have your scenic lighting on all of the time, it's advisable to install easily accessible on-off toggle or paddle switches under the front edge of the layout or on the layout fascia. This not only helps extend bulb life, it makes troubleshooting easier.

Installing interior lighting

If you want to install lights in a building, there are a number of questions to consider. Do you want lights to show in all windows or should some remain dark? With illumination, will you be able to see enough of the inside to make interior detailing necessary? Are the structure walls opaque enough to prevent the building from glowing? How will you reach the bulbs if you need to replace them? Do you want to remove the building from the layout for routine maintenance or display? The answers to these questions will influence how you build the structure.

Typically not all rooms in a building are illuminated at one time. For example, a residence may have some first floor lights and few upstairs lights on early in the evening. To create this effect in a model structure, interior walls or baffles have to be installed to partition the light, **3**.

Without interior lighting, it's difficult to see inside a structure. When you add lights, the building's interior is visible and details need to be added, **4**.

If the structure walls are made of plastic or any material that isn't opaque, paint the inside walls

Wires from miniature light bulbs can also be soldered to this self-adhesive tape, designed for stained-glass windows. The wires are easier to conceal if the tape is mounted to the underside of the roof.

black and then the desired wall color. It's wise to make the roof or floor of the building removable so the bulbs can be easily replaced if one burns out.

Making structures easily accessible is also handy if you want to install a terminal block or small plug on the wires running into the structure. However, make sure the seams are tight, otherwise there will be light leaks.

Lighting larger structures, especially commercial and industrial enterprises, requires many bulbs. Running a pair of wires to each bulb can create a potential rat's nest of wiring that may be visible through the windows. An alternative is to use self-adhesive copper foil tape, **5**, which is used in the construction of stained-glass windows and by doll-

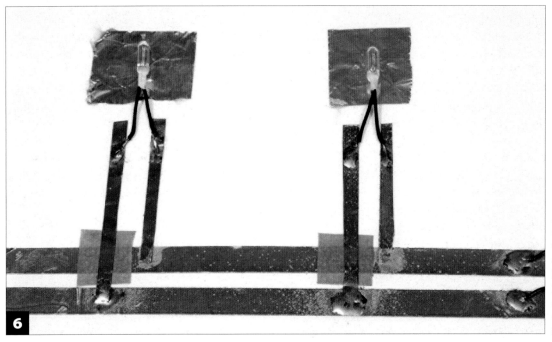

Blue masking tape insulates the crossing of two strips of copper foil tape. The primary electrical feeds, bulb leads, and junctions between two pieces of copper foil are connected with solder.

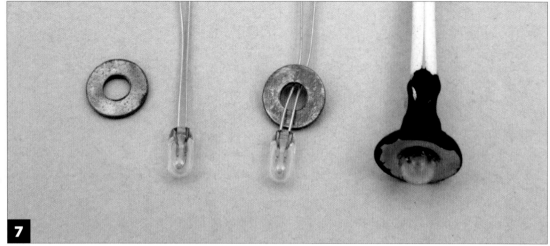

When precise detail isn't required, you can make exterior lamps by cementing a No. 2 washer on a grain-of-rice bulb. Paul applied layers of thick cyanoacrylate adhesive (CA) to give the shade its basic shape. **7**

Brawa makes an assortment of street lights that plug into flush-mounted pin sockets. Since the sockets are spring loaded, if the pole is bumped, it's not likely to break. **8**
Jim Forbes photo

house hobbyists. The ¼"-wide tape can be split in half when fewer than five bulbs are in the circuit. The tape can be run throughout the structure, **3**, **6**, and wires can be soldered to the tape. It can also be painted to match interior walls.

When installing lights, wire them in parallel. Assuming adequate current, lamps wired in parallel will not dim as you add more bulbs. It's also easy to extend a parallel circuit through a building, especially with copper foil tape. If a foil path crosses over the opposing lead, place a piece of non-conducting tape between the two strips of foil to prevent a short circuit, **6**.

Exterior lighting

Yard lights and lights over doorways and under canopies add to the overall scenic lighting effect because they illuminate a wider area. Doorway or porch lights can be a bulb with the wires stuck through the structure wall. You can either paint the top of the bulb to simulate a fixture or add a stamped metal shade such as the ones available from Campbell Scale Models (brass) and Ngineer-

ing (aluminum). Alternatively, you can put a No. 2 washer over a bulb and build up a shade using thick cyanoacrylate adhesive (CA), **7**.

Bare bulbs can be shielded on canopies with the canopy roof. For large-area illumination, a variety of lights on posts and poles are available in virtually any style desired and in many scales. Brawa and Walthers offer streetlights that plug into flush-mounted pin sockets, **8**, which makes installation easy. The sockets are spring loaded, so if the poles are bumped, they're less likely to break.

Each Brawa light also includes a small plug that looks like a manhole cover. This makes it easier to conceal the socket should you need to remove the light for maintenance, layout photography, or any other reason.

Light up the night

In addition to the scenic lighting techniques covered here, you can add illuminated signs, working traffic lights, and vehicle headlights and taillights. Special-effect circuits that simulate a flickering fire and the flash of a welding torch are also available. These

Lighting suppliers

All Electronics

149 Oxnard St.
Van Nuys, CA 91411
www.allelectronics.com
Products: Bulbs, LEDs, and power supplies

Brawa

P.O. Box 1274
Uferstrasse 26-28
73625 Remshalden, Germany
www.brawa.de/en
Products: Street lights and lighting accessories

Busch

Heidelberger Strasse 26
D-68519 Viernheim, Germany
www.busch-model.com/english.htm
Products: Animated lighting and vehicle lights

Circuitron

211 RocBaar Dr.
Romeoville, IL 60446
www.circuitron.com
Products: Bulbs, LEDs, and special lighting circuits

Delphi Creativity Group

3380 E. Jolly Rd.
Lansing, MI 48910
www.delphiglass.com
Product: Copper foil tape

Evan Designs

P.O. Box 2044
Broomfield, CO 80038
www.modeltrainsoftware.com
Products: LEDs and special-effect lighting kits

Gebr. Faller GmbH

Kreuzstrasse 9
78148 Gütenbach, Germany
www.faller.de
Products: Bulbs, LEDs, and power supplies

GRS Micro Liting

32 Wedlock Dr. SE
Rochester, MN 55904
www.grsmicroliting.com
Products: Floresta bulbs, vehicle lighting kits,
    strobes, and flashers

Micro-Mark

340 Snyder Ave.
Berkeley Heights, NJ 07922
www.micromark.com
Product: Bulbs

Miniatronics

561-K Acorn St.
Deer Park, NY 11729
www.miniatronics.com
Products: Bulbs, street lights, neon signs, and
    power supplies

Mouser Electronics

1000 N. Main St.
Mansfield, TX 76083
www.mouser.com
Products: Bulbs, power supplies, and electronic
    components

Model Power

180 Smith St.
Farmingdale, NY 11735
www.modelpower.com
Products: Assorted bulbs

Ngineering

20024 N.E. Bridled Rd.
Battle Ground, WA 98604
www.ngineering.com
Products: Miniature LEDs, lighting accessories, and
    power supplies

Parts Express

www.parts-express.com
Products: LEDs, power supplies, and small bulbs

Ram Track

229 E. Rollins Rd.
Round Lake Beach, IL 60073
www.ramrcandramtrack.com
Products: LEDs and lighting kits

Scale Shops

713 Vista Way
Prescott, AZ 86303
scaleshops.com
Products: LEDs and wiring supplies

Walthers

P.O. Box 3039
Milwaukee, WI 53201
www.walthers.com
Products: Working traffic lights and street lamps

circuits can enhance a campfire scene or the inside of a mechanic shop or industrial building.

Though some advance planning is required, scenic lighting can enhance the realism of a model railroad. The ultimate payoff is the drama of watching trains operate through the soft glow of the lights.

Author Paul Dolkos thanks Richard Daniels for sharing his experiences with scenic lighting and Jim Brewer and Bill Day for opening up their home layouts for photography.

Photos by the author

16 Painted power

By D. Derek Verner

Conductive paint lets you illuminate streetlights and other details without wires.

Imagine being able to add lighting to details and accessories without having to worry about concealing wires. Conductive paint, a metal-bearing paint used in the electronics industry for repairing printed-circuit (PC) boards, lets us do just that.

Getting started

Sources for conductive paints are listed in the box on page 72; sources for LEDs, bulbs, and other products are listed in Chapter 15 (page 69). The CircuitWorks pen, **1**, made by Planned Products, is about the handiest source of conductive paint. It is available from many electronics dealers.

Let's start by providing illumination to the three-piece styrene lampposts made by Campbell, shown in **2**. Figure **3** shows how to do it. The terminal posts offer a means of mounting and supply power to the lamppost. Heat the brass rods at one end before pressing them into the holes. This creates a firm mechanical connection. Trim off the protruding nipple at the top of the mast and cut notches with a hobby knife as shown.

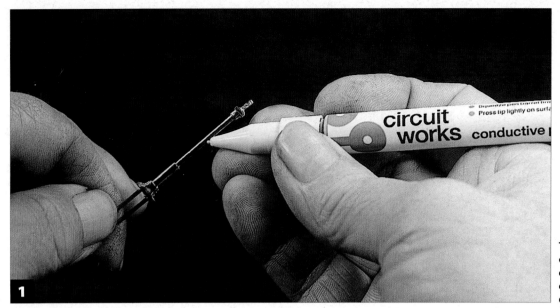

1

The CircuitWorks conductive pen is the easiest way to apply conductive paint to details.

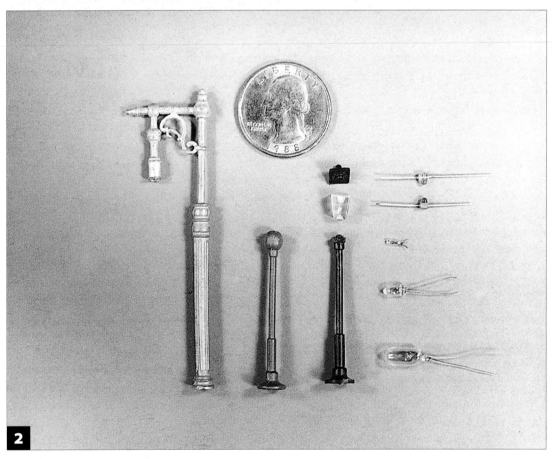

2

Various brands and types of metal and plastic lampposts can be illuminated using conductive paints. The light sources shown at right include a standard LED, Hewlett-Packard low-current LED, Cir-Kit Concepts miniature bulb, and two other small bulbs.

I've found the Cir-Kit Concepts 1.5-volt lamps work very well. They have insulated flexible leads that must be removed for use here. Since the lamp is so tiny, it can easily get lost. To prevent this, wrap the glass envelope with a temporary handle of masking tape.

Use a soldering iron to carefully unsolder the bulb. The insulating material at the base of the bulb will also soften with the heat. To make sure you don't short out the wires by inadvertently soldering them together, spread the leads in opposite directions and apply tension while unsoldering them. Clean the rest of the insulating material from the wires. Bend the wires as shown in **3**, and use five-minute epoxy to secure them in the notches. Place the clear lantern head in position and allow the

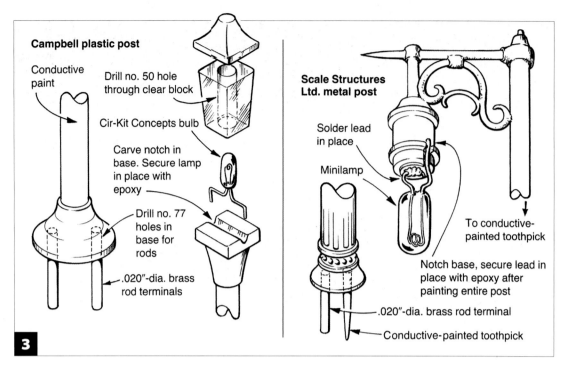

Campbell plastic post

Conductive paint

Drill no. 50 hole through clear block

Cir-Kit Concepts bulb

Carve notch in base. Secure lamp in place with epoxy

Drill no. 77 holes in base for rods

.020"-dia. brass rod terminals

Scale Structures Ltd. metal post

Solder lead in place

Minilamp

To conductive-painted toothpick

Notch base, secure lead in place with epoxy after painting entire post

.020"-dia. brass rod terminal

Conductive-painted toothpick

3

adhesive to cure. Examine the head of the lamppost; if necessary, scrape off excess epoxy covering the surface of the wires.

As shown in **1**, paint a trace of conductive pigment from each wire of the bulb to one of the brass rods in the base. The paint usually flows well. If you experience difficulty, unscrew the head and dip a small paintbrush into the pen's reservoir. You can make the traces as wide as you like, but be sure to keep them from touching one another. Test the assembly by applying 1.5 volts to the rods. If all is well, finish the lamppost by painting it the color of your choice.

The other plastic lamppost shown in the photos is one supplied in a number of structure kits. I treated it in a similar fashion, except I cut off the globe. I

replaced it with a miniature bulb and topped it with a punched-out metal disk.

Metal lampposts

Metal castings, such as the Scale Structures Ltd. lamppost shown in **2**, can also be used. The casting itself serves as one conductor to the lamp and, after an insulating coat of paint, the second conductor is painted on.

Add one brass rod terminal as with the plastic post. As fig. **3** shows, drill a second hole, insert a length of toothpick, and secure it in place with epoxy. This, when coated with conductive paint, will serve as the second input terminal.

File a notch on one side of the globe base and solder one lead from the lamp into the depression, **3**. Paint the entire lamppost casting with an acrylic paint, such as Polly Scale, and give the other lead from the lamp several coats as well. Allow the paint to dry thoroughly, and glue the painted lead into the notch with epoxy.

The paint should insulate the wire from the casting. Check to see that this is the case by scraping the paint (and any epoxy) from the outer surface of the wire and testing it with an ohmmeter. There should be a few ohms of resistance (the bulb) between the brass terminal rod and the scraped portion of the painted wire lead.

If the resistance checks out, apply a trace of conductive paint from the scraped lead down to and covering the toothpick. Finish the lamp as with the plastic one. For the lamp in the photos I added a

Sources for materials

CircuitWorks conductive pen
ITW Chemtronics
www.chemtronics.com

Nickel Print, Silver Print
Nickel Print is a nickel-bearing conductive paint with a conductivity of 5 to 6 ohms per square centimeter, and Silver Print is a silver-bearing conductive paint with a conductivity of 0.1 ohms per square centimeter
GC Electronics; sold by Willy's Electronics (and others)
willyselectronics.com

1.5V, 15mA Micro-lamps (part Nos. CK-1010-13, black wires, and CK-101-14, white wires)
Cir-Kit Concepts Inc.
cirkitconcepts.com

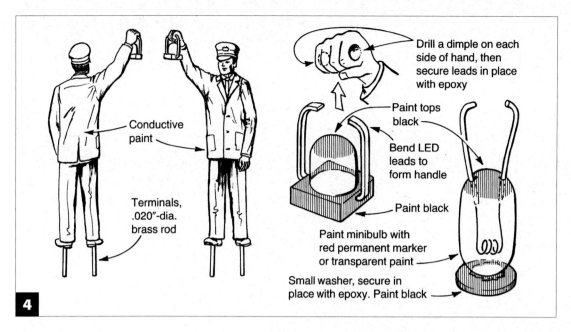

Drill a dimple on each side of hand, then secure leads in place with epoxy

Paint tops black

Bend LED leads to form handle

Paint black

Paint minibulb with red permanent marker or transparent paint

Small washer, secure in place with epoxy. Paint black

Conductive paint

Terminals, .020"-dia. brass rod

4

plastic-bead globe taken from a dime-store necklace. I drilled it out and slipped it over the exposed bulb.

Figures

These principles can be applied to flashlights and lanterns held by your layout's miniature inhabitants, **4**. The fellow in the photo on page 70 who's holding a small boy by the scruff of the neck and holding a lighted flashlight in his left hand is the usher from my Lido Theater, which is shown on page 90. Figure 4 shows how to do it. Insert a brass rod into each foot of the figure and prepare the bulb or LED by bending the leads as shown.

LEDs and miniature lamps

Many types of miniature and subminiature lamps and LEDs are suitable for use with painted power. Of interest are low-current LEDs, which I used for all the hand lanterns. These LEDs draw only 4 milliamps, compared to the 30 to 40mA of an average LED. Narrow painted traces, particularly nickel or copper paint, can't carry much current without heating up, so the small current requirement is a bonus. These LEDs are designed to operate on 5 volts, but a dropping resistor should be used if operated at a higher-than-rated voltage. A 1.8K-ohm resistor in series with the LED will light it at close to its rated current on 12 volts.

The other subminiature LED in **2** is an ordinary type, requiring a dropping resistor. Its base, however, is round and may look more like a railroad lantern.

The smallest lamp in **2** is the Cir-Kit Concepts bulb after its leads have been unsoldered. The others are available from various electronics suppliers.

They're available in many different sizes and voltage ratings and are much less expensive than lamps bought in a hobby shop. Miniature 50- and 100-lamp Christmas tree strings are excellent sources of low-voltage miniature lamps. If you wait until the post-holiday sales, you can get a bargain. They have pointed tips that make them unsuitable for some purposes, but the price is right.

Both LEDs and incandescent lamps can be operated on AC or DC, but I prefer AC for two reasons. First, all other things being equal, incandescent lamps have a longer life on AC. Second, low-voltage transformers are cheaper than DC power supplies.

Power to the people

All that remains is to deliver the required power to the brass terminals. I drill appropriately sized and spaced holes in the terrain, insert the rods, and solder feeder wires from under the layout. If you choose this method, be sure to use some sort of heat sink or the plastic may deform. A close examination of the figure with the lantern at his side will show what looks like a club foot—I didn't use a heat sink.

An alternative is to use small alligator clips. Use the insulated ones such as those available from Radio Shack. This will allow you to remove the item for servicing or place it in a new location. Clips are also easy to use, which is important since soldering to a silver-coated toothpick or sprue is difficult at best. Another option is to recess small pieces of brass tubing into your terrain, forming plug-in sockets.

Whatever your choice, be sure to try painted power for people, signal heads, vehicles, lampposts, and whatever else your imagination can dream up.

17 Pickup lights and a campfire

By Lionel Strang

It's a beautiful summer night, and John Brown and Bruce Wilson, a couple of drifters down on their luck, don't seem too worried about the arrival of the local authorities.

In this chapter we're going to build something for your brother-in-law Tom. You know Tom—he's the one who comes over to visit and always wants to see your trains but doesn't know anything about model railroading. So as a special treat for Tom (or anyone else with an untrained eye—sorry, I couldn't resist) we're going to build a small animated scene.

To animate means to bring something to life, usually by adding motion—a feature scale layouts usually lack except for the trains themselves. In this case the animation is nothing more than a flickering light simulating a campfire, but it's amazing how much life this brings to the scene. I saw the hobo campfire kit (No. GRS2000) from GRS Micro Lighting (grsmicroliting.com) at a local hobby shop and thought it would please Tom.

The kit includes two painted figures, several white-metal detail castings, and a diorama base with rocks and a campfire into which you insert a small light that when wired to the included circuit board flickers to simulate fire.

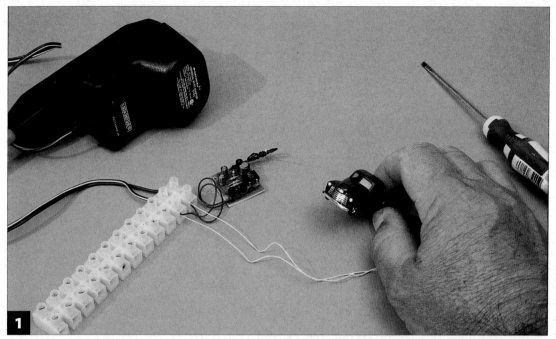

Always check that components like light bulbs are functioning before building a kit or installing items on a layout.

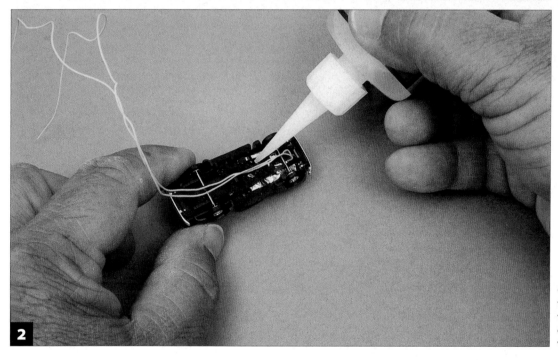

Gluing the wires to the center of the truck's frame made it easier to position the vehicle.

To complete the scene, I added a 1950 Chevrolet pickup truck (Busch No. 5643) with working headlights and taillights. Busch produces a wide variety of high-quality plastic automobile and truck models of North American and European prototypes, many with working lights. If you want to add lights to a vehicle you already have on your layout, GRS offers a lighting kit for this as well, part No. 1012.

Are the lights on?

Before starting to assemble the kit, I checked to see that both the "flame lamp" for the campfire and the lights on the truck worked. I was especially concerned that all the lights on the truck were in working order because it's never a good idea to drive around at night with one or both headlights out.

To test the lights I used a small Radio Shack variable-voltage transformer connected to one side of a terminal strip and the lights for the campfire and truck to the other side, **1**. This also gave me a chance to familiarize myself with all the parts.

Everything was in working order, but I felt that the leads for the truck, **2**, were a little short. To make them easier to work with I added about a foot

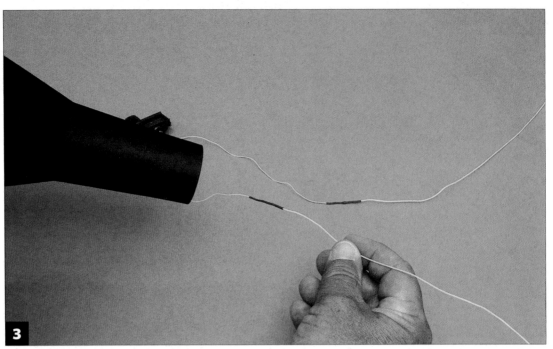

3

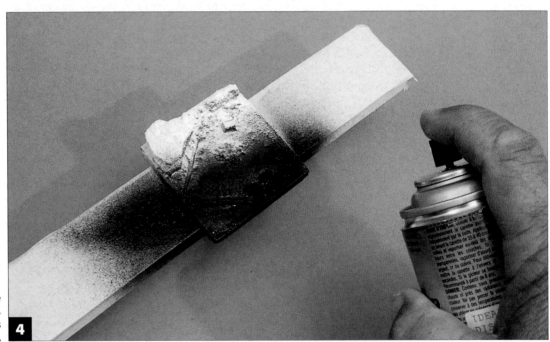

4

of No. 24 wire to each. I soldered the extensions onto the original wires then added ¾₄" heat-shrink tubing to cover the exposed wire at the joint, **3**. Adding heat-shrink tubing is simple as long as you use the correct size. As a rule, the tubing will shrink to about half its original size. Use just enough tubing to extend ¼" to ½" past both ends of the splice. After the tubing is on it's a good idea to recheck the lights.

Assembly and painting

After testing the lights, I drilled the hole in the campfire for the flame lamp. The instructions call for a ¹⁄₁₆" hole in the campfire casting and a ³⁄₃₂" hole through the layout, but I used a ³⁄₃₂" bit for both holes and was pleased to have a little extra room for the flame lamp.

I then washed the campfire casting in warm soapy water to remove the mold release. The casting is a modern, water-based polyester resin that is odor-free and takes paint well. First I spray-painted the entire casting with Testor's Flat Black paint in an aerosol can (No. 1249), **4**. Whenever you're using spray paints of any kind make sure you're in a well-ventilated area.

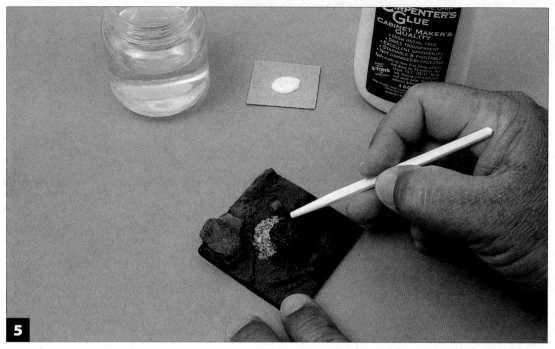

5

By brushing the glue onto the base, you can control where the ground foam will stick.

Once the black was dry, I painted the rocks using a combination of raw sienna, raw umber, burnt umber, and gray artist's acrylics (available at any art store). Buy the inexpensive ones; you don't need expensive paints for coloring rocks. I painted the logs around the campfire with Polly Scale Roof Brown.

Next it was time to add some ground cover around the campfire. I brushed on some diluted yellow glue, **5**, and, using a small spoon, lightly spread a mixture of Woodland Scenics earth and green grass ground foam on top, **6**. After allowing the glue to dry, I removed the excess by turning the casting on its side and lightly tapping it.

After I finished painting the campfire scene I painted the white-metal detail castings and glued the two figures in place.

Setting the scene

Now I placed the almost-complete scene on the layout. I inserted the flame lamp into the casting and held it in place using a very small amount of silicone caulk on the underside of the layout. I fastened the circuit board to the underside of the layout with a small screw. Be careful not to over-tighten it or you can damage the board.

I drilled a ¼" hole for the wires from the truck and fed them down from the top, positioning the truck directly over the hole. Finally, I blended the diorama base into the surrounding scene with ground foam, trees, and the additional detail castings.

You can control the lights with a simple on-off switch like I did, or if you're a little more adventur-

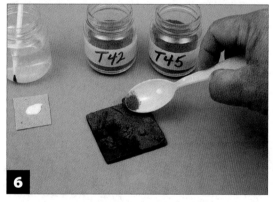

6

A small spoon makes the perfect applicator for sprinkling ground foam in tight locations.

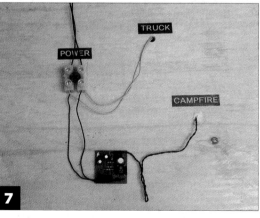

7

It's a good idea to label all wiring so later you can easily identify which wire is which.

ous you could control them with a light detection system so that when you dim the lights in your train room your campfire will spring to life. Label all wiring, **7**, to make troubleshooting easier.

I'm all set now for the next visit from Tom. When he asks me if I've been workin' on the railroad, I'll show him my campfire scene.

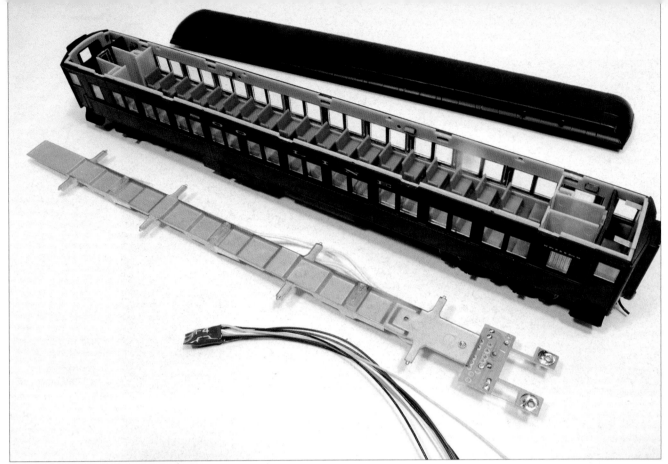

Photos by the author

18 Light passenger car interiors with DCC

By Mike Polsgrove

Mike Polsgrove added DCC-controlled interior lighting to this Walthers HO scale heavyweight passenger car. Using a decoder allows lights to be easily turned on and off.

If you have a Digital Command Control layout, the constant track voltage will allow you to have constant lighting in passengers cars whether your train is making a station stop or rolling down the tracks.

I added DCC-operated interior lighting to an HO Walthers heavyweight passenger car. The techniques can be easily adapted for use in most other cars. Most passenger car models now come equipped with electrical contacts for interior lighting. If a model doesn't have contacts, you can modify most plastic trucks by adding metal wheelsets and pickup wipers.

The track voltage provided by a booster varies depending on the DCC system, but most range from 12-16 volts (V). The most accurate way to determine the voltage is by measuring it.

Though most digital voltmeters aren't designed to measure a DCC signal, you can get a rough estimate of the voltage using the AC setting. Some DCC systems provide an internal DC measuring point. There are also external circuits and meters designed specifically for DCC that could give you exact figures, but that's usually not necessary.

Light bulbs will operate on either DC or the AC signal of a DCC system. If you use an 18V bulb connected directly across the rails, you'll likely be happy with the results.

LEDs may also be used to light passenger car interiors, but they won't operate on AC. To use them you'll need to use a bridge rectifier and a current-limiting resistor.

Walthers passenger cars come equipped with factory-installed electrical pickups, and the firm sells separate lighting kits for both DC and DCC. The kits are easy to install—just remove the roof and set the light bar in place.

The DC kit (No. 933-1087) uses a 5V regulator to lower the voltage. This provides constant lighting if the track voltage is above 6V. The DCC version (No. 933-1088), which I used, has three bulbs wired in series to equally divide the voltage. On a typical 14V DCC system, each bulb runs on a just under 5V.

I wanted the ability to turn lights on and off, so I added a decoder to each car. I chose a Digitrax TF4 function-only decoder because it's compact and has four function outputs. You can use just about any decoder that has function outputs.

The Walthers light bar has two rivets that make contact with copper strips at one end to provide track power to the top of the car, **1**. A small printed-circuit (PC) board connects the lights in series.

I removed all the bulb wires from the PC board and soldered one wire from each bulb to an unused section of the PC board, **1**. I soldered the decoder's blue wire (the lighting common) to the PC board as well, connecting it to the three bulb wires already there. I soldered the red and black decoder wires to the wires from the PC board's contact rivets.

The bulbs need to match the output voltage from the decoder—I needed to drop the voltage about 7V. The function-output voltage can be measured directly with a DC voltmeter when the decoder is connected to the track and the function is turned on. The blue wire is positive and the function outputs are negative.

Measure the current a bulb draws by placing a multimeter in series with the bulb and powering it from a DC power pack set to 12V. The Walthers bulbs draw about 30mA. Make sure a decoder's function outputs can provide the necessary current for your bulbs.

Using Ohm's Law, I calculated that in order to drop 7V at 30mA (7/.030), I needed about a 250Ω resistor. My original calculation of the bulb voltage was based on a 14V DCC system. I figured that the bulbs were capable of handling a few more volts

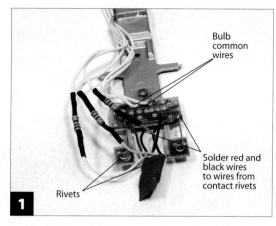

1

The Walthers light bar has two rivets that make contact with copper strips to provide track power to the top of the car. Mike soldered the red and black decoder wires to the wires from the PC board's contact rivets.

Bulb common wires

Solder red and black wires to wires from contact rivets

Rivets

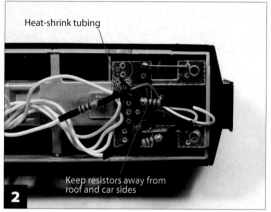

2

Heat-shrink tubing

Keep resistors away from roof and car sides

After successfully testing the light bar, Mike installed it and reassembled the passenger car. He covered any bare wires with heat-shrink tubing to prevent a short circuit.

than I'd calculated, so I used 220Ω resistors. I did one more calculation before applying the power.

To prevent the resistor from burning up, the power (watt) rating must be above the calculated power. To calculate power, square the current and multiply the result by the resistor value. In this case, (.030 x .030) x 220 = .198, or approximately 200mW. Since that's less than 250mW (¼W) it was safe to use the resistor. Be aware that the closer the working power is to the rated power, the hotter the resistor will get. As a precaution, I mounted the resistors so they wouldn't contact any plastic parts of the model.

The decoder's white wire is function 1 (F1), yellow is F2, green F3, and violet F4. I soldered 220Ω dropping resistors to the white, yellow, and green wires and covered the connections with shrink tubing, **2**. (Don't cover the resistor!) I soldered the other side of the resistors to the open wires on the bulbs, also adding shrink tubing. I then trimmed off the decoder's unneeded violet wire. I tested my wiring by connecting the rivets directly to the track with test clip, then installed the light bar and reassembled the car.

I programmed the decoder's address to the train number, which allows turning all of a train's lighting on with one address. For individual control, program the decoder's address to the car number.

19 Train-order signals with DCC

By Mike Polsgrove

Mike Polsgrove uses Digital Command Control to operate the train-order signals at depots on his HO scale Soo Line layout. This allows the dispatcher to control the signals remotely without having to run control wires to each station.

I needed train-order signals at stations on my HO Soo Line layout. To avoid running wires from each depot to the dispatcher's desk, I wired the signals with Digital Command Control using a Digitrax TF4 function-only decoder.

My Soo Line-style signals are made by Custom Signal Systems (www.customsignalsystems.com). Any signal using LEDs will work the same way.

I attached a terminal strip and a piece of perfboard to a small piece of hardboard. I used double-sided foam tape to mount the decoders, **1**. The

LEDs require 1KΩ resistors, which I mounted on the perfboard.

Both decoders are wired identically. The red, black, and blue wires are connected directly to terminals on the barrier strip. The other wires are connected to one side of each resistor. On the TF4, the white wire is controlled by function (F) 1 on a DCC throttle, the yellow wire by F2, the green wire F3, and the purple wire F4. The purple wire is unused.

After I wired the panel, I programmed its decoders using my NCE DCC system. The westbound signal is programmed to the station's milepost with the number 1 appended. The eastbound signal has the number 2 appended.

I mounted the panel under the layout. The red and black wires go to the track power. Each blue wire from the decoder is attached to the common anode wire of the signal it controls. I connected the white wire's resistor to the signal wire connected to the green LED. This allows F1 to control the green LED. The yellow wire's resistor goes to the yellow diode and the green wire to the red diode.

A DCC throttle can now control the signals, but I wanted a control panel with toggle switches. I'd previously used the NCE Mini Panel to control the turnouts in one of my staging yards. I planned on using a Mini Panel to control a staging yard that's next to my dispatcher's desk. The panel has plenty of inputs for both, so I wired my train-order signal control panel to the inputs of the NCE Mini Panel.

The Mini Panel has 31 inputs and is designed for creating control panels and other control functions. When an input is grounded, a series of DCC commands are sent through the NCE cab bus to the command station and then out the power booster to the track. Since I used mobile decoders, I needed to send locomotive commands.

The Mini Panel is capable of sending locomotive and stationary decoder commands. It uses the NCE cab bus to send commands to the command station, so it can only be used with an NCE system.

To build my panel, I used a double-pole double-throw (DPDT) center-off switch to control each signal head (one for the eastbound signal and one for westbound). I used one pole of the DPDT switch for the green and red indicators. I wired the center terminal to ground and each of the other terminals to separate inputs. I used red wire for the red signal input and green wire for the green signal input, **2**.

When the switch is thrown in one direction, the red input is grounded; in the other direction, the green input is grounded. The center-off position must ground the yellow input. To do this, the team at NCE recommended a circuit consisting of an unused input and a single NPN transistor (RadioShack No. 276-2058), **3**.

A diagram on the box identifies the transister's base, emitter, and collector. The other pole of the toggle has the center terminal connected to the base of the transistor. The other two terminals are connected to the ground on the switch. The base of the transistor connects to an unused input of the Mini Panel. The collector is attached to another input, and the emitter is connected to the ground of the

1

Mike did most of the wiring for his signals at the workbench. By building this sub-panel, he limited the amount of under-the-layout wiring.

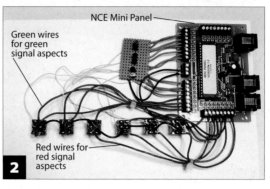

2

Mike color-coded the project by using red and green wires to coordinate with the colors of the signal aspects. This makes troubleshooting easier.

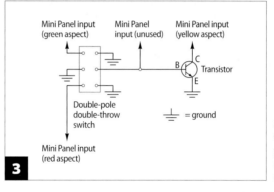

3

In this circuit, the transistor grounds the yellow input when the switch is in the center-off position.

Mini Panel. Each yellow signal uses two inputs, one of which is programmed.

With the Mini Panel wired, I programmed each input individually with NCE's ProCab. When an input is grounded, the Mini Panel executes a sequence of four commands. Inputs can be linked together to increase the number of commands.

Input No. 1 is the yellow aspect of the westbound signal, so the program consisted of two steps. The first command is to select the decoder, in this case 2811. The second command was to turn on function F2. The function command controls four functions at a time, so I made sure the green (F1) and the red (F3) functions were off.

Input No. 13 is the green aspect of the westbound signal. The first command in the sequence is to again select decoder 2811. The second command is to turn on F1. I programmed all other inputs the same way.

The panel is now ready to connect permanently to the NCE cab bus and signal. Additional signals can be added at any time just by tying them in to the track bus.

20 Light up the night with neon

By D. Derek Verner

"Neon" signs, colored with fluorescent paint and lit by ultraviolet (UV) light, add life to nighttime scenes.

Neon signs are familiar sights in every city and town. From the sputtering "EATS" sign flickering in the darkness alongside a desolate stretch of highway to the gaudy "Strip" in Las Vegas, neon signs have become a traditional part of our landscape. They date back farther than you might think, as they were introduced in 1910.

Prototype neon signs consist of glass tubing, ¼" to ⅝" in diameter, bent to shape and filled with neon or mixtures of other rare gasses at reduced pressure. Electrodes at the ends of each section of tubing are connected to a high-voltage transformer which causes the gasses to ionize and give off light. The color of the light is a function of the choice of gasses and color and coating of the tubing.

Modeling neon signs

I've found the best and least expensive way to capture the effect of neon is by using fluorescent paint illuminated by ultraviolet (UV) light. "Black light" lamps, **1**, are available from large electrical supply dealers and range in size from a 48"-long, 40-watt

1

"Black lights" are available in many sizes. The black tubes are designated "BLB," and the white one is designated "BL." Since BL tubes also emit visible light, only BLB lamps are usable for modeling. Commercial black light sources, like the one at left, are not recommended because they produce harmful short-wave UV light as well as the harmless long-wave light produced by the BLB lamps.

tube to a 5¼"-long, 4-watt tube. They operate in a manner similar to fluorescent lamps.

Fixtures for these tubes differ in only one respect from any other fluorescent fixture: The reflector is chrome-plated instead of painted white. The shiny surface redirects UV light from the back side so that it isn't wasted. A painted surface will absorb most of this light. Simply covering a standard reflector with aluminum duct tape or aluminum foil (shiny side out) will work fine.

Fluorescent paint is available in a wide range of colors. It's sold in craft, hobby, and hardware stores in bottles and spray cans. I used Testor's fluorescent model paints for most of the signs in the photos. This type of paint appears very bright even without special lighting because it reacts to the UV light that's already present in most light sources. For modeling purposes it makes our signs appear lit even in daylight scenes without UV lamps.

Sources for lettering

Except for small window signs and some skeleton roof signs, most neon signs follow one of the forms shown in **2**. This is because businesses want the sign to be visible in daylight as well as at night, when the real impact of neon signs comes across.

At first, the logical way to form model signs appears to be to shape them from thin wire. However, several attempts to do that produced results that I felt were less than successful. The lower "Crown

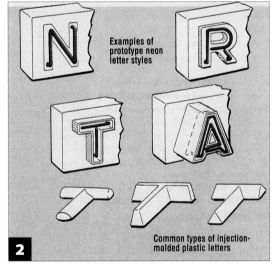

Examples of prototype neon letter styles

Common types of injection-molded plastic letters

2

Prototype neon tubing usually runs over painted sign lettering, and is sometimes outlined or framed in. Injection-molded styrene letters can be rounded, angled, or have a flat top surface.

Hotel" sign in **3** shows the results. It's very difficult to form properly proportioned letters by hand. An ideal solution (manufacturers take note) would be to have signs photoetched from suitable artwork.

Using small plastic letters is much easier. The Slater's line of injection-molded letters is among the best known, with many sizes available (you can see them online at slatersplastikard.com). Other lettering of various styles and sizes can be found in office-supply stores and from plastics dealers. Cast-metal letters are generally not as suitable because they cannot be cemented with plastic solvent.

Several plastic structure kits made for the international market have usable letters. The "Pace Freight,"

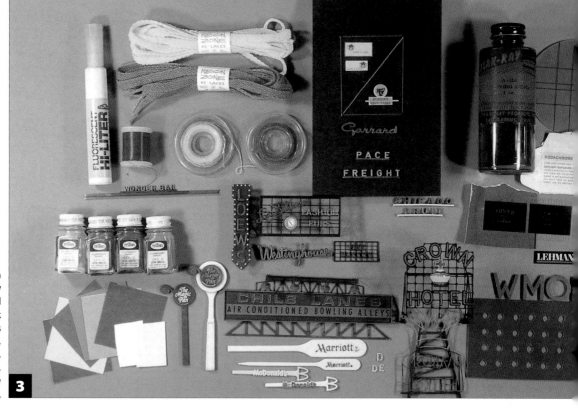

These common materials take on new life when exposed to UV light. Look for plastic letters as well as stir sticks, fluorescent paper, fluorescent thread, and other raw materials.

3

"Wonder Bar," and "Chicago Fruit" signs in **3** came from signs supplied with such kits. Since they're sold in many countries, they frequently include the same words in several languages, offering anagram and Scrabble fans a challenge to see what English words can be made from the letters supplied.

Injection-molded plastic letters usually have one of the three cross sections shown in **2**. For modeling, the best shape is the truncated triangle. This is because, in order to mimic the prototype sign formats and reduce the width of the letter strokes, we will light up only the narrow front surface of the letters. Letters with a curved cross section are the least suitable, as they require the entire letter to be illuminated. However, they can be used to model the type of illuminated sign that uses vacuum-formed letters lit from behind by fluorescent tubes.

Letters with a triangular cross section can be used, but it's difficult to paint the sharp front edge. To do this, pour a small puddle of paint on a sheet of glass and dip the letter in so that only the front touches the paint. Another method is to use a fluorescent marking pen, such as the one shown at upper left in **3**. These pens are easier to control than a brush and can coat the sharp edge with ease.

For fluorescent paints to light up brightly they must be applied over a white surface. If the letters are cast in another color, the area where the fluores-

cent paint will be applied should first be painted flat white.

Keep your eyes open for stir (swizzle) sticks, condiment forks, nameplates, plastic cup lids, and other items with bas-relief or three-dimensional letters, logos, and shapes. The "Magic Pan," "Westinghouse," "Garrard," "McDonald's," "Marriott," and "Lady Baltimore" signs in **3** are from such sources.

Figure **4** shows several typical sign designs. Skeleton roof signs generally have some sort of grid or framework to which the sign is affixed. The "Lady Baltimore" sign in **3** was mounted on a Grandt Line window casting, and the hand-formed "Crown Hotel" sign was mounted on a frame made from Plastruct angle pieces. The other "Crown Hotel" sign is mounted on a piece of wire screen. The solder blobs at the intersections of the wires can be filed down if they seem objectionable.

In recent years Bar Mills and Blair Line have both released a wide variety of laser-cut wood kits for rooftop signs in N through O scales, many of which include separate letters. These can be illuminated with the techniques shown here. The letters and logos can also be used to make other styles of signs.

Letters mounted against a wall, such as "Lulu's Lunchroom" and "Lacy's Variety" are simply cemented to an appropriately colored background, as are the projection and upright sign letters.

Other materials

Fluorescent paper is available in many colors from art and office supply stores. The paper can be used as glowing backgrounds for signs in which the lettering is done with black dry-transfer letters. That's how the lower half of the "Chilb Lanes" bowling alley sign was done.

One way to make window and other signs is to use the paper (or the paint) behind a film negative, like the "Tony's Fruits and Vegetables" and "Lehman" signs in **3**. [The high-contrast Kodalith film Derek used is no longer available; a good substitute is to print out designs on clear acetate transparencies. Graphic art houses can also print out negatives from your artwork or computer files.]

Make sure the paper is in tight contact with the negative, or this technique won't work properly. Place small dots of Walthers Goo or contact cement on the opaque areas of the negative to bind it closely to the paper.

Decals can be mounted on fluorescent paper if the decal film is the full size of the backing paper. Decals not made this way won't work well because the edge of the film will be visible. The "Lorie's Gifts" sign illustrates this method. Before applying the decal, spray the paper with a sealant such as Testor's Glosscote.

Many art supply stores carry fluorescent dry-transfer letters. The upper half of the "Chilb Lanes" sign was made using these. Even though the letters have an under-printing of white pigment, they work better if mounted on a light but contrasting color background rather than the dark one shown. Note that this sign is supposedly frontlit by floodlights. This technique works as well for signs supposedly backlit.

Another way of modeling a sign lit by floodlights is to use transparent ultra-violet ink. Commonly used for security hand stamps, this type of UV ink appears clear under normal light but shows up in various tints under UV light. The Living Light shown in **3** is long out of production, but other types are available from UV Products (uvp.com) and other suppliers.

Ordinary paper, including many signs offered by model suppliers, is sometimes fluorescent without special treatment. Two rectangles of typing paper are shown on top of the color swatches in **3**. One glows brightly under UV, the other does not. That's because manufacturers often put fluorescent dyes into paper and cardboard products to make them appear whiter and brighter.

You may be surprised at how many products around the house glow under the influence of UV light. This can be a drawback if you use UV lighting on your layout. You may find that some of your modeling materials glow brightly when you don't

SKELETON ROOF SIGN

WALL AND WINDOW SIGNS

Bob's FISH

LIVE BAIT To Go

PROJECTION SIGN

BILLIARDS BALL 8

UPRIGHT SIGN

Joe's PARK $1.00

4

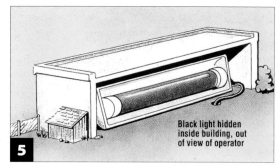

Black light hidden inside building, out of view of operator

5

A building can hide a small UV lamp and fixture.

want them to. If this happens, you may have to repaint the item in non-fluorescent paint. Some dealers in UV products market a transparent liquid that will stop the transmission of UV light so the item no longer glows.

Other fluorescent items in **3** include elastic, thread, yarn, and shoelaces. All the fluorescent fabric materials I've seen are made of fine filaments that are bundled together. These can be unraveled and re-grouped into bundles as thin as you like. They're excellent for modeling straight lengths of neon tubing to outline signs or serve as accent lighting on movie marquees. The lines shown on the piece of construction paper were made this way. Fluorescent drafting tape (as narrow as 1/32") is also available.

Some plastics are available in fluorescent colors, and the photos show some acrylic pieces and molded letters. The letters are large for most purposes, but they work well for call letters mounted atop a broadcasting station.

Placing the UV lamps

If you plan to use fluorescent materials extensively on your layout, you may want to flood an entire scene with UV light by suspending large (40-watt) fixtures overhead. If you do, be sure to take full advantage of the benefits of UV by using the pigments and materials for other lighting effects. How about stars and a glowing moon for your night sky? You could light street lamps, vehicle and train lights, and windows. Even the windows in flat backgrounds can be lighted with paint or small squares of fluorescent paper.

If you want to light only a few signs or areas, the smaller-sized lamps can be concealed within or behind other structures, **5**. Remember that these lights operate on 110 volts and should be wired accordingly.

Try some of the techniques outlined in this chapter. When visitors admire your handiwork, you can be assured that it's a good sign.

21 Fiber optics in model railroading

By Lee Vande Visse

For several years I've been exploring ways to apply fiber optics to model railroading. That's why I built the city scene above.

But first some background: Fiber optics have been around since the 1950s. They look like monofilament nylon fishing line, but internally the similarity quickly ends. As shown in **1**, these fibers are actually made in two parts, a glass core and the plastic sheath surrounding it.

Light shining into one end passes through the core and out the other end, following any bends

in the fiber. A marble, rolling down a hallway and glancing off the walls, is a loose analogy. Both the core and the cladding must be of the highest optical clarity for this to work, and the terms "glass" and "plastic" are oversimplifications for the exotic materials actually used.

The crucial factor is that the interface between the two materials must act to constantly reflect light back into the core and prevent its escape or absorption. The benefit to the hobby is that we now have "light tubes" which have an infinite life, are reason-

The author built this scene to experiment with fiber optics. The show is spectacular. The marquee lights chase one another, and those on the Kola sign build in a sequence. Fiber optics generate no heat, so they can be mounted in plastic signs with no fear of damage.

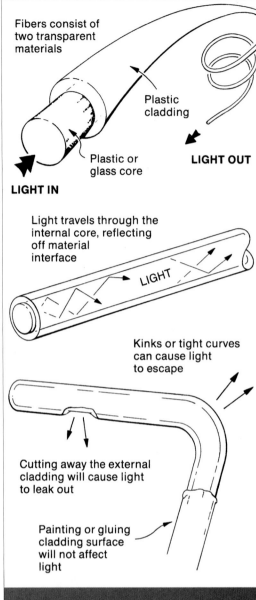

Fibers consist of two transparent materials

Plastic cladding

Plastic or glass core

LIGHT OUT

LIGHT IN

Light travels through the internal core, reflecting off material interface

LIGHT

Kinks or tight curves can cause light to escape

Cutting away the external cladding will cause light to leak out

Painting or gluing cladding surface will not affect light

The principles of using fiber optics are simple: Shine a light into one end, and light will pass through (even long distances) to the other end.

1

ably durable, and can be used almost without regard to length limitations.

Two factors, however, can decrease the effectiveness of the fibers. Despite their appearance they cannot be handled like fishing line. A kink can crush the glass core, and the light will disperse at the point of damage. Before using any strand, test it for bright spots by placing a light bulb at one end. Bright spots along the fiber can indicate damage and should be eliminated.

Also, the more a fiber loops and turns, the more light it will lose. A gradual turn or two will not noticeably affect the output, but several tight 360-degree turns will definitely make the final light dimmer. The best teacher is experimentation.

Fiber optics come in a variety of diameters. I've accumulated many, ranging from some about the thickness of hair taken from an old mood lamp to some as large as the handle of a needle file. By far the most useful have been strands approximately .020" in diameter.

You can find fiber optics through many outlets, including science supply and surplus stores and online through many electronics, optics, and hobby dealers including Edmund Scientifics (www.scientificsonline.com), www.nationalartcraft.com, and www.hobbylinc.com.

Fiber optics can also be scavenged from items such as old mood lamps, tabletop Christmas trees, and other crafts. Keep your eyes open at yard and garage sales and antique stores.

Light sources

The easiest way to transmit light with fiber optics is to position a single bulb next to the end of the fiber in a remote area and then lead the fiber through the layout to its eventual end.

You'll quickly notice that the total usable light will always be limited to the amount of light that strikes the fiber at its initial cross section. This can be enhanced somewhat by beading the end with a flame or soldering iron, **2**. This technique is also called flame-polishing and will improve the performance up to a point. You can also form a bead at the emitting end to create a light bulb shape.

Unless you use an extremely strong light source, fiber optics are poor illuminators, so don't try to use them to light up an area. If you wish to light the inside of a building, the best bet is still grain-of-wheat bulbs or their equivalent. But if you're going to be looking directly at the end of the fiber, the light is strong, clear, and the same color as the source.

A Christmas miracle

Prior to last Christmas, I had been working on a method to make lights blink, **3**. I wanted to use this for fiber optics signs, billboards, and such in a city scene. At the time it seemed a good solution. The idea was to periodically block the light reaching the fibers by passing the sides of a slotted cup in front of the source light.

A motor would slowly rotate the cup, and the placement and size of the slots, coordinated with the speed of the rotation, would determine the eventual appearance of the blinking at the end. Derek Verner used a variation of this method to add chase lights to his scratchbuilt Lido Theater, **4**, which he built in the 1970s (with an article on it in the March 1976 *Model Railroader*).

I built three of these contraptions, and then came Christmas. Inspiration is one of the great feelings in life—a bright flash that instantly informs you you've been a dope the whole time. It came when I was looking at a Christmas tree in a store. The lights were blinking in sequence, one after another down the line. Then it hit me! Here was my blinking light source!

I immediately scrapped every bit of complicated machinery on my workbench and began working on the scene you see pictured. As I said, these lights flashed in sequence, with a definite forward motion and an in-line control to determine the tempo. Prior to discovering this product, I thought building a theater marquee with fiber optic chase lights was possible but just too complicated. But these lights seemed to be the perfect solution.

But there was more! I could change the bulbs. The bulbs are normal Christmas tree twinkle lights available during the season. The normal sequence for the string was red-green-yellow-blue, but I could make them go red-red-blue-blue, or white-white, or whatever. With this ability I could make signs that go on and off, alternate between colors, or twinkle—anything. The potential was beginning to seem endless to me. By this time I had also learned how to combine fibers into bundles, so that the possibilities were verging on the astronomical.

Implementation

The two methods I used with the most success for aligning the fibers with the bulbs are shown in **5**. The most important things to remember are that you should have an easy way to change the bulb and that the filament of the bulb should align with the fibers as closely as possible.

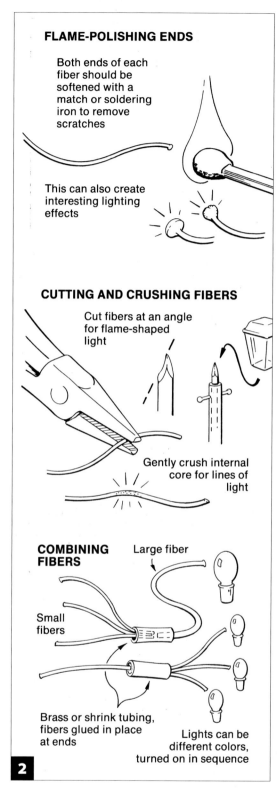

FLAME-POLISHING ENDS

Both ends of each fiber should be softened with a match or soldering iron to remove scratches

This can also create interesting lighting effects

CUTTING AND CRUSHING FIBERS

Cut fibers at an angle for flame-shaped light

Gently crush internal core for lines of light

COMBINING FIBERS

Large fiber

Small fibers

Brass or shrink tubing, fibers glued in place at ends

Lights can be different colors, turned on in sequence

2

Heating the end of a fiber optic strand provides a realistic bulb shape.

When I have aligned the fibers correctly, the light coming out the other end is almost alarmingly bright. I have even found myself thinking that the light must certainly burn out the fiber. This type of thinking comes from years of working with grain-of-wheat bulbs hooked to a transformer and is embarrassingly wrong!

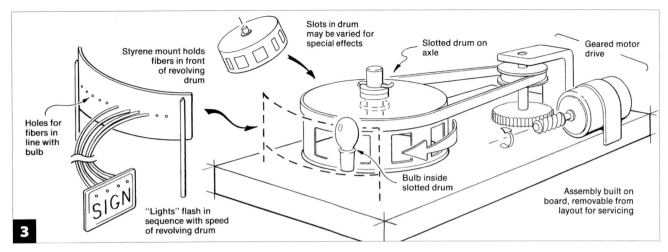

Styrene mount holds fibers in front of revolving drum

Slots in drum may be varied for special effects

Slotted drum on axle

Geared motor drive

Holes for fibers in line with bulb

Bulb inside slotted drum

"Lights" flash in sequence with speed of revolving drum

Assembly built on board, removable from layout for servicing

3

A rotating device can be used to make a chase-style marquee, but an easier method is to use a strand of twinkling or chase-style holiday lights.

The focal point of the display I made is the theater marquee. All those lights are really the tips of more than 100 individual fibers, and the effect is exciting. The colored lights march around the perimeter of the sign just as on the real thing.

Each fiber measures .020" in diameter, although I did flare the end of each just a bit with a match to create a bulb effect and keep the filament from pulling back through the hole. By comparison, the smallest bulb I have ever seen is the Pacific Fast Mail Micro-Miniature, which measures .040". Besides being large, bulbs also emit heat, melt plastic, and have

two wires that must be hooked up. On the marquee that would mean 200 wires, and then you'd need the electronics to control the sign—but by now I have made my point. With fiber optics, construction is a far simpler matter of stringing the fibers through the holes and back to the appropriate bulbs.

Reliability

Within my pike I also have a string of generic twinkly lights, the kind that have been around for years. The whole string blinks in unison, the pace being set by one master bulb. As with the chase light strings,

D. Derek Verner scratchbuilt this HO movie theater with working chase lights made from fiber optics, using a motor mechanism to light them in sequence. The usher with flashlight at left is described by Derek on page 70.

4

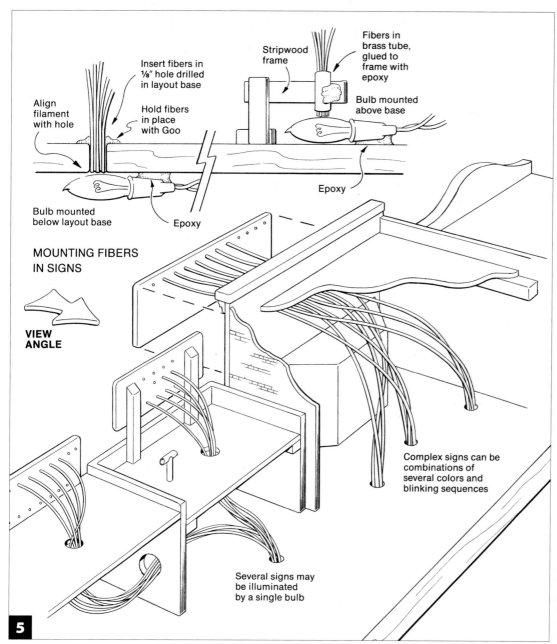

Insert fibers in ⅛" hole drilled in layout base

Fibers in brass tube, glued to frame with epoxy

Stripwood frame

Align filament with hole

Hold fibers in place with Goo

Bulb mounted above base

Bulb mounted below layout base

Epoxy

Epoxy

MOUNTING FIBERS IN SIGNS

VIEW ANGLE

Complex signs can be combinations of several colors and blinking sequences

Several signs may be illuminated by a single bulb

5

You can light large bundles of fiber optics with a single bulb. You may have to get creative with under-layout bulb mounting.

these are wired by the manufacturer in series, so one bulb going bad means the whole string goes without a hint of where the fault lies.

After approximately 60 hours of operation, one bulb did burn out, followed shortly by another. I blame this mostly on the quality. These strings cost all of $2.50. I was able to find the offending bulbs and replace them and have since wired test leads into these strings to help isolate future problems.

The chase light strings seem to be much more durable. I have yet to experience my first failure after more than 100 hours of operation. The price of these strings (about $20) reflects the additional quality, and I use only the bulbs from other chase light strings in altering colors in the string on the layout.

Ponder the possibilities

Finally there is another idea, which I have not yet worked out but may be of interest to those inventive souls who can't leave the workshop tidy. Consider this: Embedded crushed cores of parallel fibers just below the surface of an Enviro-Tex cast-resin lake would make sparkling wavelets in the surface. Lead the fibers back to random sparkling white lights, and see what happens.

There's more you can do with these fibers. The sky's the limit, and speaking of skies, how about twinkling stars that come out at night when you turn down the room lights, or flashing aircraft warning lights on your taller structures, or vehicle headlights and taillights? Just let your imagination roll.

22 Layouts should be seen ... and heard!

By David Popp

Layout realism is enhanced with soft under-layout sounds. This is David Popp's N scale Naugatuck Valley layout, but the same principles apply to large and small layouts in any scale.

Of the five senses, after sight, hearing has the next biggest role to play in model railroading. Adding sound to a layout provides an extra layer of reality: When the scaled-down objects you're looking at make the noises you'd expect them to make, the modeled world becomes more realistic. With that idea in mind, I set out to add sound to the recently completed portions of my N scale layout.

You may think adding sound to your model railroad would be difficult, but guess again. All the projects shown here involve installing small, self-

powered media satellite speakers under the benchwork. And when you use high-quality sound recordings, the sound appears to come from everywhere.

Although each of these projects involves amplified speakers, the best results come from running them at "scale volume"—which means low. Real locomotives or clock tower chimes are loud when you stand right next to them, but that isn't how you relate to them as models on your layout. Even when you view your models at eye-level, you're still at least several-hundred scale feet away – so the volume needs to be scaled down accordingly. This way your models will sound as realistic as they look.

Self-contained system

One way to add sound to your model railroad quickly is to use off-the-shelf, self-contained components. Model Rectifier Corp. (MRC), Noch, and a few others, make ready-to-use layout sound modules. The MRC Sound Station system, **1**, comes with two powered speakers and a handheld control unit. This particular system includes sounds for city and country scenes, but MRC also offers a railroad version.

The unit features two types of digital-sound files—continuous and short-duration. Continuous files repeat over and over when activated and include sounds such as stream noises, passing traffic, and gently falling rain. The MRC system also features an assortment of button-activated short-duration sounds which play set patterns. This system includes sounds such as a dog barking, a car horn, a siren, and farm animals.

Sound-effects CDs

By using an inexpensive compact disk player and a set of media satellite speakers under the layout or in the scenery, you can add continuous background sound almost as quickly as with a self-contained system, **2**. (Sound-effects records, tapes, and CDs have been around for a long time, so this method is really nothing new.)

After doing a little research, I came across a company called Fantasonics Engineering (www.fantasonics.com). The firm has provided sound for theme park attractions and museum displays for years and is now applying those techniques to its Scale Magic line for model railroad sound products. These are richly layered sound effects tracks, designed to represent sounds from different locations and industries, and are era specific. After trying all of the firm's sample sounds on its website, I ordered the "Big City" and "Roundhouse/yard"disks for the World War II era, the period closest to what I model.

According to Jim Wells from Fantasonics, the sound-effects tracks are created from a combination of actual recordings and studio-engineered sounds. On the city disk, along with the constant hum of traffic, at various times just a few of the distinct sounds you can pick out include crows, a Salvation Army band, a clock tower and carillon, pieces of conversations from passers-by, gusts of wind, and train crossing bells.

1 The MRC Sound Station is an easy way to quickly install ambient sounds to a layout.

2 A common portable CD player with external speakers can play a variety of sound effects from commercial or homemade disks.

Adding these sounds to a layout is easy. As shown in the photo, you can use an inexpensive CD player and speakers. Fantasonics includes a detailed 33-page how-to booklet with your first purchase, which explains speaker positioning and how to get the most from scale sound effects on your layout.

The Fantasonics CDs include multiple tracks, each of which has a different mix of sound effects and background noises. You can set most CD players to play continuously, repeat one track, or randomly choose between all the tracks on a disk. Considering that each track is approximately 6 or 7 minutes long, these disks offer a great variety of background sounds.

The Dream Player from Pricom Designs provides high-quality interactive sound effects.

3

A card reader attached to a PC pulls sound files from memory cards.

4

Interactive sound modules

Though CD sound effects are easy to use, they have at least one drawback. Every time you turn on your layout, you need to reprogram the play selections. Also, the CD option doesn't allow for any real interactive features—once it's playing, it stays that way.

An option that avoids those issues is an interactive sound module. Pricom Design (www.pricom.com) makes a solid-state audio playback system called the Dream Player, **3**. This player is designed for use with model railroads and museum displays and provides high-quality stereo sound. You can use the Dream Player in a variety of ways to add as much or as little interactive sound to your layout as you wish. And unlike the CD player, when you turn on the Dream

Player, it knows exactly what it should be doing.

The system plays .wav sound files stored on SD flash memory cards. Using a simple card reader, **4**, and a PC, you can load your own .wav files on the card (up to four tracks). Pricom offers an assortment of sound files on its Web site as free downloads. I tried these and enjoyed the ocean sound so much that I let it play on my office computer for a week!

Dream Players require an amplified speaker system, and any powered satellite speaker set will work. I purchased two 14-watt sets with sub-woofers for my players from Best Buy for about $35 each and got excellent results, **5**.

I used two Dream Players and speaker sets on my layout, one under the city of Waterbury and another under the rural river scene on the other end of the railroad. For the river scene, I ordered a 512MG SD card from Fantasonics loaded with its "Creeks and Streams" sounds. I set this player to start playing when I turn on power to the layout, and it loops the 40-minute track continuously.

For the Waterbury player, I loaded three different .wav files on the card. The first two are from tracks on the Scale Magic "Big City" CD. The third comes from the "Roundhouse/yard" disk, which I used to represent the industrial sounds for the brass-manufacturing plants in Waterbury. After converting these files to the .wav format, I placed them on the card as tracks one, two, and three. (I left the fourth track open for the time being.)

The Dream Player can have as many as four external triggers (one for each track). These triggers can be push buttons, motion sensors, photo cells, occupancy detectors, or even Digital Command Control decoders. I used three momentary contact switches (Radio Shack No. 275-646) for this player, mounting them at various places on the fascia around the city, **6**.

When an operator pushes one of the two buttons on the city side of the peninsula, he gets city noises. If he moves to switch the industrial side of town and pushes that button, the Dream Player fades out the city track and then starts the industry track. Fantasonics engineered the industry track to include city noises in the background, so operators on either side get some of the proper sounds.

The Dream Players work wonderfully, and the sounds carry around the room enough that they blend well. When you're standing by the river scene, every so often you can hear the chimes of a distant clock tower from the city's player, which is a great effect!

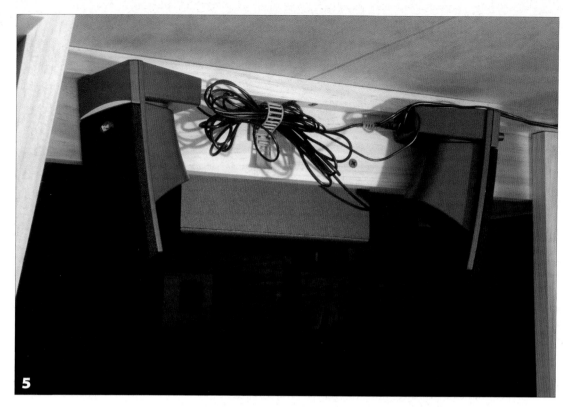

A small speaker system with subwoofer is mounted under the layout to provide the layout sounds.

5

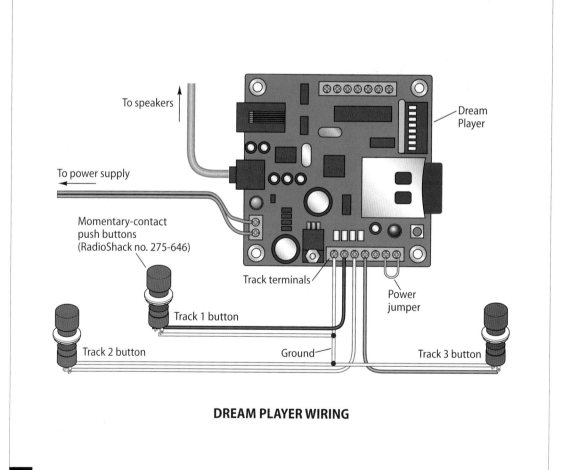

To speakers

To power supply

Momentary-contact push buttons (RadioShack no. 275-646)

Dream Player

Track terminals

Power jumper

Track 1 button

Track 2 button

Ground

Track 3 button

DREAM PLAYER WIRING

6

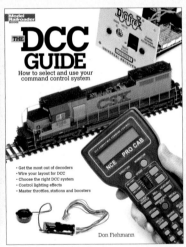
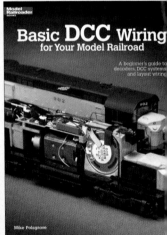